The Fireplace Book

The Fireplace Book
Roxana McDonald

The Architectural Press:
London

First published in 1984 by The Architectural Press Ltd,
9 Queen Anne's Gate, London SW1H 9BY

British Library Cataloguing in Publication Data

McDonald, Roxana
    The fireplace book.
    1. Chimneys—Great Britain   2. Fireplaces—Great Britain
    3. Dwellings—Great Britain—Heating and ventilation
    I. Title
    728   NA3040

    ISBN 0-85139-835-9

Cover illustration credits

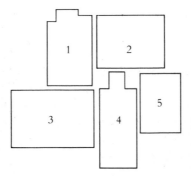

1, 2 Roxana McDonald
   3 National Monuments
     Record
   4 British Architectural
     Library/RIBA
   5 Institute of Agricultural
     History and Museum of
     English Rural Life, University
     of Reading

Typeset by Phoenix Photosetting, Chatham
Printed in Great Britain by R. J. Acford, Chichester, Sussex

Contents

Foreword

'Hearth' and 'home' – the two words, in the English mind, are indissolubly wed. Social as well as technical change have made it difficult to recall what has been a way of life for centuries – yet, blackened timbers of surviving medieval roofs still speak eloquently of the lost hearth below, and many urban skylines in Britain still display seemingly limitless ranks of chimneys – vivid memories of the bygone age of the fireplace.

The domestic interior of today strives for its missing focus, and those whose pleasure it is to rescue and adapt older houses rejoice at the occasional discovery, behind boarding, of an attractive cast-iron hob grate or sometimes a larger, more capacious, earlier fireplace-opening within which this was later set. Occasionally, indeed, a more challenging and puzzling mass of old brickwork yields up a cavernous ingle-nook, complete with herringbone fireback and spanned by a brave oak beam, scarred by wiping off the red hot poker which mulled an Englishman's beer. Truly in its range of variety and historical anecdote, no single element of the house is more evocative.

But there is more to fireplaces than sheer nostalgia; and their many practical advantages are being rediscovered. To start with, the energy crisis has stressed the necessity of re-evaluating solid-fuel heating, and this often involves reinstating the fireplace. The momentum gained during recent years in protecting our historic heritage has increased our understanding and skill in the techniques of preserving old structures.

Fireplaces have a major role to play in solving the intricate puzzles of restoring historic buildings: they are invaluable for dating houses, they give spinal support to old structures, and their shafts provide the much needed ventilation that is so often lacking in modern interiors, with such disastrous effects on the fabric of old buildings. In some instances disused fireplaces and flues have provided the answer, when dealing with the incongruous demands of modern comforts – from hiding air conditioning and electrical ducts to housing custom-made lifts. In new buildings, too, the fireplace has its worthy place.

Roxana McDonald's interest in fireplaces was kindled (if that is the right word in the present context) while a postgraduate student of the Course in Building Conservation at the Architectural Association in London. The Architectural Press has done us all a favour in encouraging her to develop the subject, and then in presenting it for the pleasure of other architects, for the stimulation of the student and the interest of ourselves, her readers.

The practical guidance with which she concludes will help many owners of old houses towards a more sympathetic enjoyment of their prize, and towards the sensitive care of both hearth and home.

Donald W. Insall OBE FSA FRIBA FRTPI SPDipl (Hons)

Part I
Historical restoration

1
The development of architectural features

The architectural history of the house would be difficult to follow separated from its focal point: the hearth. Similarly, it would be virtually impossible to look at the development of the fireplace without relating it to the building that contains it. The intention in this book is to take a brief view of the development of the fireplace, pointing the way to clues to dating a building, bearing in mind that an understanding of how and why fireplaces have been built at a certain point in time will help facilitate their care and use today.

Throughout history the meaning of words describing the fireplace have changed, interestingly and consistently reflecting its evolution. For example, the word 'chimney', originally referring to the complete structure, fireplace and shaft,[1] became 'the iron chimney' meaning what we now call 'the grate', and progressively subdivided into 'the chimney-piece' or 'fire surround' (so often now regarded as part of the internal furnishings and not the building), and the flue shaft and outlet.

For the purposes of this book the word 'fireplace' will be used as referring to the whole structure, as a collective term for all its components. 'Chimney' will be employed in its modern sense of flue terminal.[2]

Saxon period (ninth to eleventh centuries)

There is no evidence that the Roman occupation had any lasting architectural effect in Britain, and whether this was due to the policy of ruthless destruction of the Saxon invaders or just to lack of impact, is hard to say. The fact remains that none of the advanced Roman methods of construction, such as brick-making, were adopted after the Romans' withdrawal. The same applies to their methods of heating.

While the Romans used a sophisticated system of underfloor hot air flues from a central furnace and charcoal braziers, the Saxons continued to use the primitive hearth fire, lit in the centre of the floor of a hut, open to the roof, through which the smoke would escape.

---

1 'Caminum' or 'cheminée' for the whole fireplace, comprising hearth, mantel, flue and chimney or for any of its parts (Salzman, 1952, p. 98).
2 For further details on nomenclature of components, see fig. 1.1 and the illustrations to the history summary on p. 55.

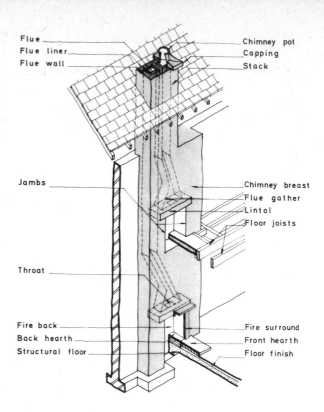

Flue
Flue liner
Flue wall

Chimney pot
Capping
Stack

Jambs

Chimney breast
Flue gather
Lintol
Floor joists

Throat

Fire back
Back hearth
Structural floor

Fire surround
Front hearth
Floor finish

1.1 Fireplace construction: terminology.

Basically timber builders, the Saxons applied their shipbuilding skills and techniques to the improvement of the indigenous turf hut, evolving it from the circular plan to a rectangular one and thus establishing the beginning of what was to become the mediaeval hall. They built timber homesteads which they shared with their cattle and food stores.[3] These were housed at one end of the building, the service end, while the living accommodation with the central hearth fire was placed at the other end (see fig. 1.2).

Norman period (1066 to twelfth century)

The Normans in their effort to consolidate their conquest of England, established themselves in stone fortresses, strong enough to resist any Saxon retaliation. A great number of castles and houses were built all over the country, with two or more storeys, in which the ground was used for storage and the upper levels for living accommodation.

Because most floors were made of timber, the central hearth position was impractical and so the wall fireplace became almost exclusively used in this type of building. This is really the origin of the fireplace as we understand it today.

However, one characteristic that differentiates the Norman fireplace is that it formed an integral part of the structure of the building. Whether scooped into the thickness of the wall as at Castle

---

3 See Addy, 1905, p. 98.

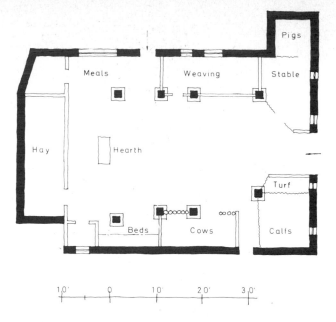

1.2 Saxon house.
a plan, *b* reconstruction view.

a

b

Hedingham (see fig. 1.3) or adjacent to it, on a hooded, corbelled platform as at Conway Castle (see fig. 1.4) it was as much part of the wall as a door opening or window. This is quite obvious when one looks at castle ruins today, where floors have fallen centuries ago and the walls stand with their fireplaces intact (see fig. 1.5).

Always a part of a side wall, the plan and shape of the fireplace itself changed as a result of efforts to improve the disposal of smoke as at Boothby Pagnell Manor House (see fig. 1.6), where the flue is no longer discharged at the side, (as at Castle Hedingham), but is carried up vertically and terminated with a tall cylindrical chimney shaft where the smoke issues at the top.

1.3 Castle Hedingham
fireplace in the State Room
(c 1130).
a plan. The shallow
semi-eliptical recess, lined with
thin Roman-type bricks is typical
of this period. The flue at this
period is often constructed to
have several outlets (two in this
case, either side of the buttress)
for smoke disposal in different
wind conditions.
b section.

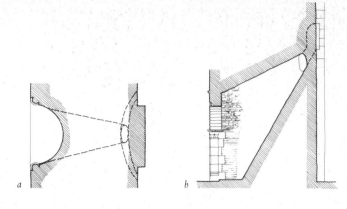

1.4 Conway Castle hooded
fireplace.

6

1.5 Donnington Castle

Gatehouse (c 1386).

a elevation view of west wall.
b flue sections (fragments of stonework found in the courtyard suggest that some of the chimneys had octagonal shafts).
c hearth detail. The hearth is of stone and the recess is lined with characteristic thin bricks.

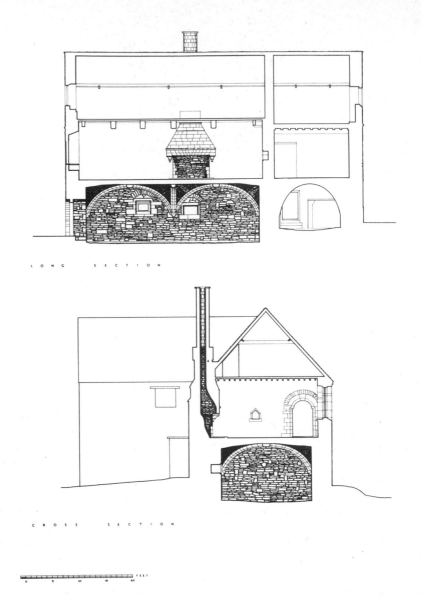

LONG SECTION

CROSS SECTION

1.6 Boothby Pagnell Manor House (*c* 1200).
Sections showing that the flue was carried out vertically and terminated with a tall cylindrical shaft issuing the smoke at the top and not the sides.

Chimney shafts, like that at Northborough Castle in Northumberland, which is octagonal in shape (see fig. 1.7), were often beautifully decorated. The decorations were functional: the projecting mouldings provided protection from rain and the crenellation reduced the effects of the wind by breaking up cross-currents (see also fig. 2.4).

Although towards the end of the Norman period the wall fireplace became extremely efficient by contemporary standards, improvements like the hood, which were to be much used in France, seem to have had little following in Britain, where they were gradually abandoned.

1.7 Northborough Castle: decorated octagonal chimney shaft.

It has been argued that hoods were often employed but, because of the use of perishable materials (plastered timber and wicker), time has extinguished any evidence of their existence. It is known from contemporary records that plastered hoods were used as cheaper versions of stone ones, for example, that ordered by Henry III for his wardrobe at Windsor.[4] However the absence of surviving associated features, such as incorporation into the wall structure and a cylindrical flue system, suggests that they did not continue to be employed in the Norman tradition. The later hoods, even when for practical reasons they had a back-up wall, operated as an inverted funnel with a louvre vent at the top, and their location in the plan of the house implies that they were used in association with the improvement of the central hearth.

The use of the Norman side wall, hearth and flue shaft system was becoming increasingly modified, and by the sixteenth century was generally forgotten. Thus in 1538, Leland expresses his wonder at the chimney arrangement in Bolton Castle built in 1380:

'One thinge I much notyd in the haulle of Bolton, how chimneys were conveyed by Tunnels made on the syds of the wauls, betwyxt the lights in the haulle; and by this means, and by no covers, is the smoke of the harthe wonder stangely conveyed.'[5]

---

4 Pipe Rolls, 20 Henry III, Turner, 1851, p. 84.
5 Cited in Addy, 1905, p. 112.

Norman kitchens

One other major change brought by the Normans was the separation of cooking from other activities. Their elaborate meals could no longer be prepared on the hall fire in the Saxon way. The sheer quantity of food required enormous fires which produced unbearable heat and smoke. (Monks at St. Swithin's House at Winchester rebelled when the number of courses at dinner was reduced from thirteen to ten.) But no Norman kitchens have survived and it is assumed that they were temporary structures.

By the end of the Norman period kitchens were built with increasing concern for the disposal of heat and smoke, and became established as separate buildings. The kitchen at Glastonbury Abbey (see fig. 1.8) is one of the finest surviving examples of this tradition. This remarkable Gothic construction, which served a household of about 300 people, is the only surviving part of the Abbot's accommodation. It consisted of four fireplaces situated one in each corner of a square plan, formed into an octagon by the pointed fireplace arches. Apart from the individual flues placed above each fire, the general ventilation was provided by a top louvre which made ingenious use of the structural support in increasing the efficiency of smoke and heat disposal.

1.8 Glastonbury Abbey
kitchen (mid-C14th).
a plan.
b external view.
The four enormous corner fireplaces were served by individual flues while the main space was ventilated by an ingenious central lantern within the roof structure.

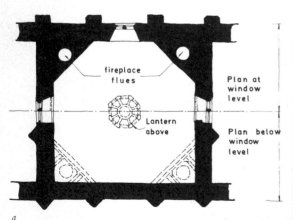

Early English and mediaeval periods (twelfth to fifteenth centuries)

After the height of the Norman period, a bifurcation occurred in the development of the house. The higher level of the social hierarchy, which maintained strong French connections, continued in broad terms to adopt and evolve the Norman way of life, while the great majority of the lower levels persisted in the Saxon tradition, adapting and improving it with the means within their reach. While this separation in development has been generally accepted in the analysis of the evolution of the house, it seems to have been overlooked in the study of fireplace development, where the difference often has been accounted for as lower-level improvisations of grander versions.

There are many possible reasons for this division in the type of fireplace: local rejection of foreign influence, lack of suitable materials, but probably the most important was lack of wealth. The Norman wall fireplace required expensive building materials and craftsmen and, once in use, consumed large amounts of fuel, as much of the heat would be lost through its external wall position. The central hearth on the other hand, was cheaper to make and use, and its location provided a more efficient way of using the heat by enabling more people to gather round and benefit from the fire, albeit with a lot more smoke. Also, for buildings constructed almost exclusively of timber, it had a safer position, with less risk of accidental fire spread.

In parallel with documented survivals of wall fireplaces from great buildings like abbeys, castles or fortified manor houses, there are many references to the wide use of the central hearth.[6]

It seems logical therefore that the development of the fireplace should be considered along these two parallel lines, until changing circumstances caused them to converge.

THE MEDIAEVAL CENTRAL HEARTH

Occasionally used even in more important households like Penshurst Place (see fig. 1.9), where it survives today as one of the last complete examples of its kind, the central hearth was commonly used in the Saxon manner in the characteristic mediaeval hall house. The similarity of the plan types and hearth position between the Saxon house and hall house is striking (see fig. 1.2, 1.10).

The aisled 'main floor' of the Saxons had developed into the hall, while the service end, used originally for stock, was reduced, as outer buildings were built for this purpose. The 'house end' on the other hand was much extended and the cross passage, previously a

---

6 William Harrison, as cited in Lloyd, 1975, p. 83, in his 1577 *Description of England* remarked:

'There was an old man yet dwelling in the village where I remain which have noted three things to be marvellously altered in England within his sound remembrance and other three things much increased. One is the multitude of chimneys lately erected, whereas in their young days there were not above two or three, if so many, in most uplandish towns (the religious houses and manor places of their lords always excepted, and peradventure some great personages), but each one made his fire against a reredos in the hall where he dined and dressed his meat.'

1.9 Penshurst Place (*c 1341–9*).
a plan.
b view of the hall and the hexagonal central hearth of tiles with a low stone curb.
c a reconstruction of what life could have been like in Penshurst Hall, around the central hearth fire (*View from The Olden Time* by Joseph Nash).

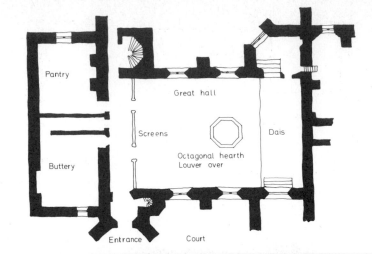

Pantry

Great hall

Screens

Octagonal hearth
Louver over

Dais

Buttery

Entrance   Court

a

b

c

12

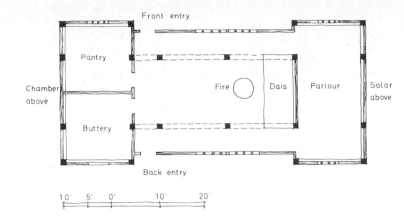

1.10 Characteristic hall House.
a plan, *b* view.

secondary access dividing the 'fire house' from the 'ox house' and providing the 'threshing floor', was now established.

The hearth, just like the Saxon one, was placed on the floor of the higher end of the hall, thus emphasizing the hierarchy of the place – the higher one's status, the closer one sat to the fire. In front of the hearth was placed a double-ended fire-dog (see fig. 1.16a) consisting of two iron uprights with spit loops and animal headcaps joined by a horizontal bar, used for the roasting of meat. The frontal fire-dog persisted until the fourteenth century when it was gradually replaced by lateral fire-dogs (see fig. 1.16b, 1.19), which were used primarily for the support of the logs forming the fire bed.

Towards the end of the middle ages steps in improving the smoke problem mark the beginning of a period of transition towards the masonry chimney. Various timber structures appeared. First as a smoke bay (see fig. 1.11b), then as a smoke hood (see fig. 1.11c), they retained the central hearth position, and later, towards the end of the sixteenth century, as brick became more commonly used, they were to be replaced by the brick chimney (see fig. 1.11d).

13

1.11 The transition to the masonry chimney.

a The original hall house.
b The smoke bay.
c The smoke hood.
d The brick chimney.

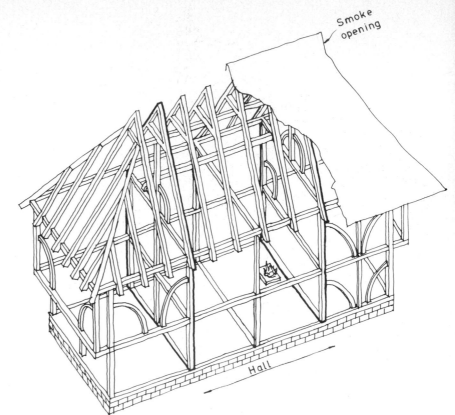

a

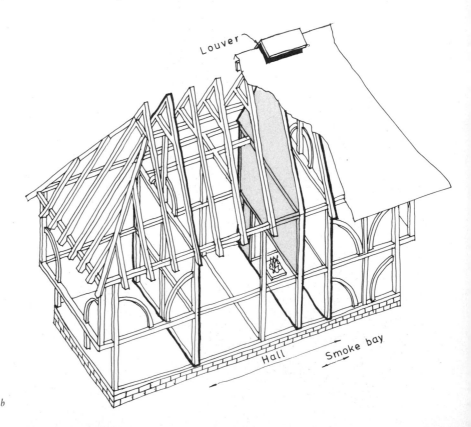

b

14

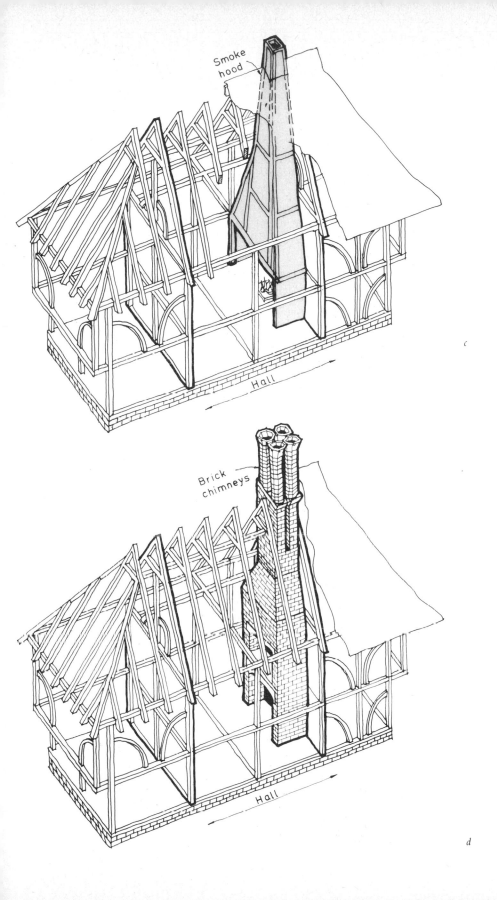

Smoke
hood

Hall

c

Brick
chimneys

Hall

d

Evidence of the central hearth fire of mediaeval halls can still be found on the roof timbers, blackened by smoke (see fig. 1.12), and there are still many examples of fire bays, hoods and central hearths in existence. In the Medicine House in Blackenden, Cheshire (fig. 1.13), a fine example of a 1513 hood and louvre top has survived remarkably unaltered, giving a clear indication of how the central hearth tradition of grouping around the fire continued.

THE MEDIAEVAL WALL FIREPLACE

During the mediaeval period great abbeys, churches and castles were being built and craftsmanship was reaching one of its highest points through the development of the Gothic style.

The construction of the wall fireplace was subject to improvement and change. Its plan location remained in the side wall but the shallow recess with the rudimentary flue scooped into the wall was gradually replaced during the thirteenth and fourteenth centuries by the hooded platform in front of the wall on which cylindrical flues were raised to stone chimneys. The hood was usually of a pyramidal shape supported by a one-stone lintel with 'joggled' ends, constructed of a stone stepped at the ends so as not to slip, as at Conway Castle (fig. 1.4), or a number of stones joggled for the whole length.

An interesting transition example can be found at Abingdon Abbey in Berkshire, where hooded fireplaces with cylindrical flues dispose of the smoke at the side and not at the top, either through the triple lancet openings at the top of the parlour chimney shaft or through openings in the wall, protected by stone baffles (see fig. 1.14).

During the fifteenth century the hood was abandoned, and a fire, entirely recessed in the wall thickness, (now purpose-built with a chimney breast), was adopted, with a pointed arch that spanned the opening, flush with the face of the wall. Such fireplaces were introduced in the side walls of a hall usually near a bay window, below the dais.

Exquisite craftsmanship was to make the fireplace reach its highest development during this period, and centuries later be the source of inspiration for the Victorian Gothic Revival. Towards the end of the century brick was rediscovered as a building material, and an increasing number of elaborate brick chimneys were beginning to be constructed, introducing what became an important feature for the buildings of the sixteenth century.

Tudor and Elizabethan period (sixteenth century)

The sixteenth century marked the start of a new era in British architecture, as the Renaissance movement began to exert an increasing influence through Italian artists brought over by Henry VIII and Cardinal Wolsey. Brick was manufactured on a larger scale and became available to the less wealthy, while at the same time, timber was beginning to become scarce. The use of oak was gradually restricted to important buildings only, and, by the end of the century,

1.12
a **Open hall** roof timber
blackened by the central hearth
shows open fire in use before the
insertion of the floor in the
double-height hall.
b **Central hearth** survival at
Old Orkney Cottage (note the
chair circle around the fire).

a

b

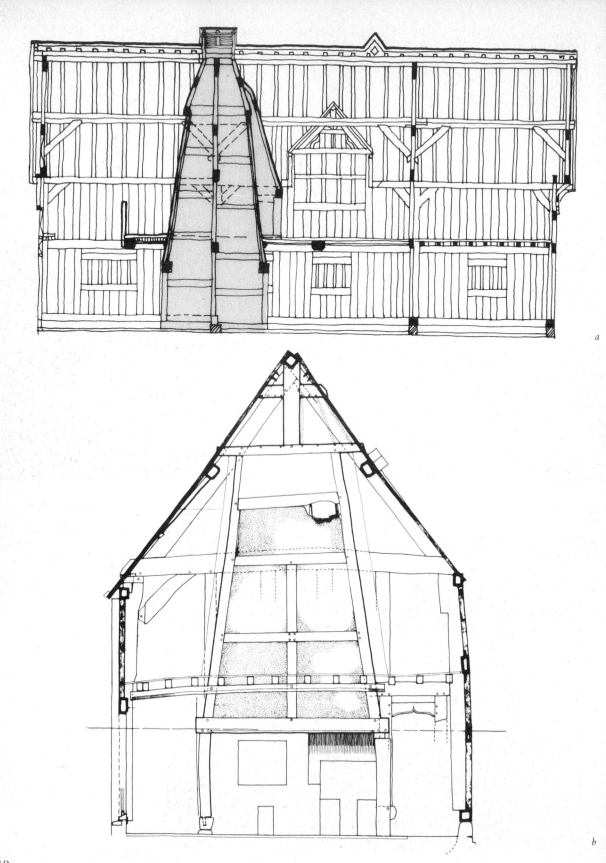

c

d

1.13 The Medicine House (1581).
a   Section through the fireplace.
b   Detail of stack framework.
c   External view, showing louvre vent in roof apex.
d   Detail of hood over the central fire on the ground floor.

1.14 Abingdon Abbey
(*c* 1260). The smoke was still disposed of through side openings: the triple lancet openings at the top of the parlour chimney shaft and the wall openings protected by stone baffles shown here on the left of the shaft's base.

coal started to be considered as an alternative fuel to wood. Each of these changes had a pronounced effect on the development of the fireplace.

THE SIXTEENTH-CENTURY CENTRAL HEARTH

In the sixteenth century the central hearth, still in use, was slowly being replaced by brick chimneys inserted in its place, quite often in the 'smoke bay' (see fig. 1.11b, d). (The central position was usually maintained, even in newly built houses.) The hall was losing its double height as floors were inserted half way up to create an upper room with a fire. The fireplace itself had become more massive, a group of two or three fires back to back often typifying this stage.

The kitchen fire and oven started to move back into the house from an outside building due to improved smoke and heat control. The following Parsonage Terrier extracts, entered in 1606, give a good indication of the change:

'Swaby (1606) 3 bays covered with thatch the whole building being contrived into Hall, 2 parlours, 3 chambers, etc. Item a kitchen of one bay and an oxhouse. . .'

'S. Willingham (1606) 3 bays built with strong timber and well covered with thatch, all the bays being chambered over, some with boards and some with clay. Three rooms – parlour, hall kitchen, the same house having also two chimneys in brick in height about three yards.'[7]

Kitchen fireplaces, sometimes in pairs, as at Hampton Court (see fig. 1.15), tended to be very wide so that long logs could be laid on iron dogs, due to the large amount of food which had to be provided at one time. Radial roasting in front of the fire was done on long spits, turned at first by hand and later by weights and pulleys (see fig. 1.17).

THE SIXTEENTH–CENTURY WALL FIREPLACE

The great house of the sixteenth century was no longer fortified, and there was more care for comfort. The classical influence introduced at this stage affected mostly the decorative treatment of the wall fireplace, rather than its plan position, which remained the same. The Tudor arch was replaced by a rectangular opening with decorated jambs and lintel.

To start with, the fireplace was not much emphasized, except perhaps for a tapestry hanging, and the wainscoting characteristic of the sixteenth century interior was continued over it. Later, as many craftsmen came to England from Italy, Flanders and Germany, the fireplace gradually became an object of display, considered as a separate exercise and no longer part of the structure as a whole.

The fire surround was for the first time emerging as an entity in its own right, incorporating orders of architecture, albeit in a way which had little relationship yet with the façade or with the rest of the general interior design elements. Early Renaissance work displayed a certain over-enthusiasm where decoration was concerned, as the traditional craftsmen were trying to handle out–of–context foreign elements (see fig. 1.18). But the iron dogs and firebacks which completed the sixteenth-century fireplace were beautifully cast with ornate decorations, and sometimes even with armorial crests, (see fig. 1,19).

Seventeenth century

The signs of change in the plan and design of the house apparent throughout the sixteenth century started to take over in a spectacular

7 Cited in Barley, 1961, p. 276.

1.15 Hampton Court kitchen
(early C16th).

**1.16 The evolution of
fire-dogs.**
a Frontal fire-dogs, which
persisted until C14th were
originally used singly in front of
the fire for meat and roasting
spits.
b Lateral fire-dogs were later
introduced to support large logs
and loops added for the spits.

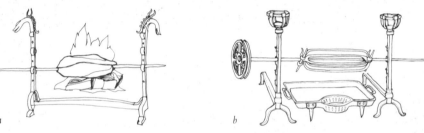

**1.17 Iron dogs and roasting
spit with turning wheel.**

1.18 Renaissance influenced chimney-piece at Fawley Court.

1.19 Examples of iron fire-dogs.

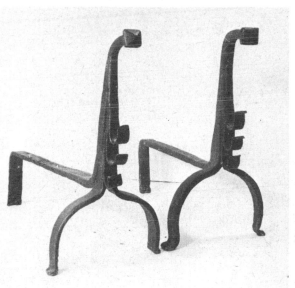

way during the seventeenth century. A completely different approach was causing a revolutionary replacement of old values. The change was reflected in the difference between Gothic and Renaissance, beautifully summed up by Nathaniel Lloyd in his *History of the English House* as 'The difference between a product of many minds, freely exercised in developing forms suggested by the materials with which they worked and a product of one highly trained and organized mind, working to rules, which imposed forms upon buildings'.

The 'highly trained and organized mind' was that of the architect, who from this time on would increasingly dominate the building scene. Needless to say, the fireplace took its share of the change, in both its parallel forms of development.

The effects were more dramatic in the case of the central hearth. Its development began to follow a less parallel line until, in the eighteenth century, it finally met and identified with that of the wall fire.

THE SEVENTEENTH–CENTURY CENTRAL HEARTH

Brick chimneys continued to be inserted around the central hearth, and the subdivision of the full-height hall by a floor was being adopted as a matter of course. The introduction of 'sea borne' coal into domestic use precipitated these insertions, as coal smoke was much more difficult to tolerate in an open hearth fire. But again, the plan location remained central, physically enclosing the hearth.

The relationship between people and the fire was also in the central hearth tradition, where the family would gather around the fire and its 'funnel' cover (see fig. 1.12b). However, when, because of the chimney insertion, the circle could not be completed in the same way, a reduced version had to be accepted: seats either side and in front of a hearth, which was backed by a brick wall protected with a cast-iron piece. In this way, the chimney-corner or ingle-nook came into being, a last vestige of centuries of tradition (see fig. 1.20a).

An alternative theory, which considers the ingle-nook to be an offshoot of the wall fireplace, is based on certain examples in smaller houses, where in an attempt to imitate more prestigious buildings, the appearance of a wall-recessed fireplace was improvised by situating the hearth in a corner (hence the ingle-nook), and, as at Tyrland's Farm, Enmore (see fig. 1.20c), with the help of a short wall at the other end this gives the impression of depth and greater wall thickness. But, as Shuffrey notes: 'although of considerable width, [they] have not sufficient height in the openings to be used as chimney corners, which appear to have been a later development'. Furthermore, their plan position was chosen in the wall-fire manner, while the majority of ingle-nooks were actually sited at the centre of a building.

Nevertheless, with increasing use of coal and the introduction of common features such as firebacks, or the basket, the demarcation between the central hearth and the wall fireplace was becoming less distinct, and, for the first time, the vernacular tradition was under serious threat. The difference between the two types became more and more of a cosmetic nature.

1681.—Chimney Corner of the Kitchen in Henley Street.

b

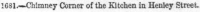

1.20a The ingle-nook— meeting point of tradition and modern building technology.

1.20b The modern kitchen range gradually took over from the traditional ingle-nook and open fire hearth.

1.20c Tyrlands Farm, Enmore, Somerset (*c* 1600). The oak beam and stone jambs are employed in a 'wall fireplace' manner over a recess created with the aid of the corner and a short wall, to give the impression of depth usually associated with thick stone walls. *Below*, plan, *Above*, elevation.

THE SEVENTEENTH-CENTURY WALL FIREPLACE

The Renaissance symbolized refinement and wealth and the upper levels of society found it irresistible. They began building their houses in the classical manner, and the designed symmetry was often achieved at the expense of logical function.

Fireplaces, too, were no longer treated simply as necessary provisions, but, due to their impact on the façade, became the subject of special aesthetic consideration and concern. Whether ingeniously grouped to produce a striking symmetrical effect or almost out of

25

view, the position of the fireplace on plan was often dictated by the design of the elevation. The aesthetic revolution of the Renaissance would have liked to sweep away the functional wall fireplace along with everything else that formed part of the Gothic tradition. But there was a problem, as none of the Italian theorists, whose books laid down strict rules for the perfect classical building, had much to say about fireplaces. The Mediterranean climate did not need them, and in Britain they became a puzzling source of embarrassment to classical designers. Two great English architects faced this dilemma during the seventeenth century, and their brilliant answers paved the way to the classical climax of eighteenth-century fireplace design.

The first was Inigo Jones (1573–1652). His revolutionary treatment of interiors amended the sixteenth century's clumsy attempts at classical detailing and established for the first time the designed chimney-piece as the focal point in the room. His Palladian designs consisted of a full-height composition of superimposed classical opening frames, often crowned by a pediment (see fig. 1.21). Constructed of carved marble or stone, they incorporated a marble mantelshelf (stone, oak or plaster in cheaper versions), a characteristic feature which was to be a source of inspiration for the designers of the eighteenth century.

The second architect to have an impact on fireplace design was Sir Christopher Wren (1632–1723), who reduced it from being the main feature of a room, to one of the elements of a composite design. In

1.21 Chimney-piece design by Inigo Jones.

1.22 King's Dressing Room, Hampton Court (*c* 1690). Note the heavy bolection surround which will become increasingly characteristic in the William and Mary period.

21

his designs the overmantel becomes part of the wall panelling (enriched in the post-Restoration period by Grinling Gibbons's superb carvings), and the opening is framed with a simple, heavy 'Bolection' moulding. Along with overmantel mirrors, the introduction of shelves for the display of china is a typical Wren feature. He also encouraged the fashion brought to England from France by Charles II, which placed fireplaces in corners (see fig. 1.22) in spite of criticism from people like John Evelyn who claimed it 'took away from the state of greater rooms'. It certainly made it difficult for people to gather round the fire in the old way, but design was winning against tradition.

During the seventeenth century fireplaces in chambers became much more common, but due to taxation they remained but a status symbol: the 1662 tax on hearths, which was raising £200,000 a year at a rate of 2 shillings for every fire (except for the poor) gives a clear indication of the numbers. However, they continued to grow, and in the eighteenth century fireplaces could be found even in church pews.

Eighteenth century

From the Restoration onwards the sense of regional propriety was weakened by the increased opportunity to travel. Land ownership was undergoing basic changes, and, with the final enclosure of the open fields, the links with the mediaeval past were completely broken.

A century of new ideas, the eighteenth century laid the foundations of the modern construction industry. The first speculative builders made their appearance, and a great number of houses were built with the help of the pattern book, which was to deal vernacular tradition the last blow. The middle class was emerging and, at the upper social levels, Lord Burlington, and other 'persons of distinction' and 'men of taste' took over architecture as 'patrons of the arts', setting the standards for elegance and refinement. In their wish to 'educate' the taste of the country, they commissioned a great number of buildings and published books on design.

James Gibbs, the author of one of the earliest of such books, clearly outlined their purpose in his introduction to his *Book of Architecture*, published in 1728:

'Such works . . . would be of use to such Gentlemen as might be concerned in building, especially in the remote parts of the country, where little or no assistance for Design can be procured'. Past building efforts 'unfortunately put in the hands of common workmen' were treated with contempt and labelled 'monuments of the Ignorance or Parsimoniousness of the owner . . . that are best pulled down'.[8]

The vast number of pattern books published, produced by Batty Langley, Isaac Ware and John Wood, to name but a few of the authors, had a tremendous impact on the plan and design of the

---

8 Cited in Lloyd, 1975, p. 130.

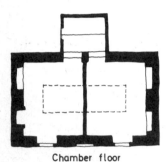

Chamber floor

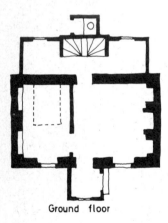

Ground floor

1.23 After John Wood's 'Cottages or Habitations of the Labourers'.
An example of C18th pattern book cottage design.

house, and slowly new buildings at all levels achieved an unprecedented uniformity of concept. The fireplace, too, was completely reconsidered. Its components, the stack and the chimney-piece, were now two completely separate entities. The first, as part of the façade, was positioned in the plan in order to achieve a symmetrical effect; the second, as part of the interior, became the subject of design and pattern books in its own right.

House plans of this period were made unmistakably 'Eighteenth Century' by their symmetrical layout, and the gable positions of the chimneys were a result of this drive for symmetry. The difference between pattern book cottage plans (see fig. 1.23) and plans of town houses or even grander examples is mostly a difference in scale, unit arrangements and numbers.

The increase in opportunity for the lower levels of society to emulate the higher was a reflection of economic and political changes, and Dr Johnson's remark, when visiting Oxford with Boswell in 1754 that: 'In old halls the fireplace was anciently always in the middle of the room, till the Whiggs removed it to one side'[9] points to this new dimension to the development of the house.

The central hearth was now a thing of the past, save in the homes of the very poor, and so was the wall fireplace in the Norman sense: both had been replaced by a fireplace representing, not a way of life, but a commodity.

Tradition died hard and, at the same time, despite the fashion and the building boom, not everyone could afford to build a completely new house. In many cases old buildings were given a face-lift with a new classical elevation, but the old fireplaces were hardly ever demolished.

The fact that Palladian elevations and chimneys have been added to an earlier building is often confirmed by the presence of a central stack, belonging to the plan of the old house. But, when houses were built afresh, the chimney stacks were kept to the gable ends in accordance with classical canons. This can be a valuable clue to the past history of a house, the presence of a centrally located chimney in conjunction with a Georgian façade often suggesting an earlier building.

The surround continued to preoccupy designers until its appearance was finalized in the style established by the Adam Brothers, (see fig. 1.24). From this point, apart from the effects of progress made in the design and manufacture of the hob grate, it remained virtually unchanged. From here on the development of the fireplace consisted of a series of technical innovations aimed at improving performance, supplemented by successive revivals of earlier decorative styles.

Towards its end, the eighteenth century became saturated with classical taste. Some started to have doubts and, like Isaac Ware, were questioning whether architects were right to 'transfer the buildings of Italy right or wrong, suited or unsuited to the purpose, into England'.[10] The signs of nostalgia were already showing, and

---

9 Cited in Wright, 1964, p. 25.
10 Ware, 1756, p. 694.

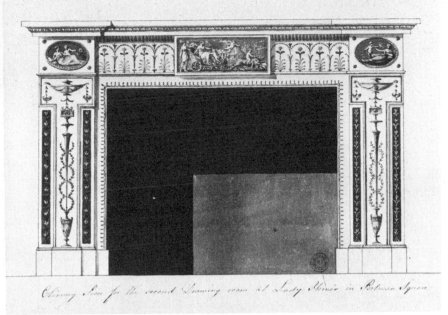

Chimney Piece for the second Drawing room at Lady Home's in Portman Square

1.24a Robert Adam's design for a chimney-piece for the dressing room in Portman Square.
1.24b The same fireplace as built.

1.24c Chimney-piece from the music room at Norfolk House, St. James's Square, now in the Victoria and Albert Museum. The marble mantel is attributed to Giovanni Battista Borra and the carving to John Cuenot, 1753–6.

'Gothick' fireplaces, like the one designed by James Wyatt in 1785 for a friend of Walpole, now in the Victoria and Albert Museum (see fig. 1.25b), were a prelude to the nineteenth-century taste for revivals.

Perhaps Victorian romanticism was the result of a subconscious need to reach back to a lost tradition after the design hiatus, but however faithfully reinstated, the products of revivals never quite achieved it. The 'chemistry' between the craftsman and his materials was lost in sterile replicas in which the material no longer suggested forms, but was being tamed into them.

Victorian period

The Industrial Revolution which characterized the nineteenth century created an age of great contrasts; extreme wealth and prosperity in parallel with squalor and poverty; the opulent architecture of country seats opposed to monotonous rows of terraced houses; great

1.25 'Gothick' examples.
a Stone chimney-piece.
b Chimney-piece designed by Wyatt, now in the Victoria and Albert Museum.

interest in the unique features of revived craft styles counteracted by mass production. But, as the Victorians were united in their readiness to reject the preceding century's extravagance as a reassurance of their own respectability, they were also united in their eagerness to employ the multitude of innovations of a century full of wonderful new ways of achieving unprecedented comfort at all levels. Never before had the people of England experienced the certainty of the Victorians and their conviction that they knew best.

The fireplace reflected the Victorian contrasts; at one end of the scale it hardly changed as part of the terraced house, while at the other end it almost re-lived its own history through the multitude of revivals which started with the 'Gothick' – a symbol of rediscovered spiritual purity (see fig. 1.25). The Regency aristocrat, as an arbiter of taste, was replaced by the rising industrialist of the middle classes, whose less discriminating tastes encouraged many poor imitations and strange mixtures of styles. Neo-Gothic and Elizabethan were thrown together in the desire to 'outdo', and the avalanche of patents and innovations only helped to make things worse. Towards the end of the nineteenth century a sense of satiety and want of identity found relief in neo-romanticism. The owner of the cast-iron framed and tiled fireplace (see fig. 1.26a) now idealized the discomforts of

a

b

1.26 Victorian fireplaces
a   Victorian fireplace with pine mantel and tile inserts.
b   Modern reproductions of a Victorian cast-iron surround.
c   Victorian register grates advertized in 'The Ironmonger', 1878.

c

Design for Fire place in Picture Gallery.   Scale 1" to one foot

the past, and the reminiscing Pre-Raphaelite paintings delighted him as did the architectural early–Renaissance revival, later replaced by the 'Queen Anne' style of Norman Shaw, W.E. Nesfield and others, (see fig. 1.27).

As the century drew to a close, exciting new discoveries, gas and electricity, were sure signs that the era of the open fire was coming to an end.

Twentieth century

By the beginning of the twentieth century, the English home had attained a degree of comfort unsurpassed anywhere in the world.

1.28 Edwardian fireplace.

Adequate heating was a high priority and every room was provided with a fireplace. In the early part of the century 'Gothick' went out of fashion and the ingle-nook became the new source of inspiration, as many architects placed importance on the fireplace, following the examples of Sir Edwin Lutyens (see fig. 1.29) and C.F.A. Voysey, (fig. 1.30), who was among the first to return to the spirit of the vernacular tradition. A distinctive new style was generated by the Art Nouveau movement, a main exponent of which was Charles Rennie Mackintosh (see fig. 1.31), but after the First World War one bland and 'clinical' styling fashion followed another, with the fireplace being reduced to a dull nonentity that succeeding generations had no qualms in discarding. The pattern of society was changing again; big house owners, no longer able to employ enough servants to stoke the fires, had to seek new methods of heating, and oil central heating and gas and electric fires finally replaced the open fire.

This, until a few years ago, would have been the end of the story. But the oil crisis and the lack of progress in finding alternative sources of energy have changed the scene and we are turning back to the open fire.

1.29 Sir Edwin Lutyens:
Cottage at Littleworth, Serle,
Surrey, 1889 showing his
characteristic treatment of
chimneys.

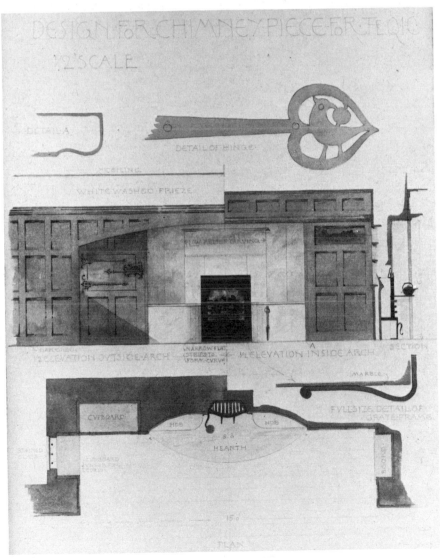

1.30 C.F.A. Voysey: Design of
chimney-piece from the 'Quarto
Imperial Club' sketches.

1.31 Fireplace designed by Charles Rennie Mackintosh now in the Victoria and Albert Museum.

2
Development of features associated with smoke disposal and fire risk

The performance of the open fire has always been hindered by two problems: the disposal of the smoke and the risk of fire. Throughout history, man's ingeniousness has produced a remarkable succession of attempts, some more successful than others, to solve both problems, all leaving their mark and influence on the appearance and development of the fireplace and chimney.

It has to be said that, until modern times, most open fires smoked, although decreasingly so. It is important to remember this when thinking of restoring an open fire, as today's standards of comfort bear no resemblance to those of the past, when people were hardy enough to tolerate smoke, draught and cold to a much larger extent than we might think (see fig. 2.1). The type of fuel used for the fire was a deciding factor in the smoke disposal saga and therefore must be considered in close association with it.

Development of features associated with smoke disposal

The diversity of ideas and methods employed in the battle against smoky fires is vast, but for the purposes of this book it is intended to identify only the major steps so as to provide a basic framework for anyone wishing to date, conserve or restore an open fire of a certain period.

Wood fires

SAXON AND NORMAN PERIODS

The Saxons' approach to the smoke problem was as simple as their way of life. The smoke from the central hearth fire had to find its way through the unsealed roof, under the eaves or through unglazed windows. Sometimes a special opening was created in the roof, and this practice was continued by the poor, especially in rural areas, until as late as the seventeenth century (see fig. 2.2).

The central hearth used during Norman times must not be imagined as a roaring bonfire. The wood was carefully chosen, seasoned and often toasted into semi-charcoal before being brought indoors in braziers. A fire of green wood was a sign of poverty. In large establishments, a hearth-keeper would ensure that the fire was properly made and maintained, which meant a 'clean fire' with very little smoke.

2.1 Illustration from 'The English House-wife' by G. Markham (1683) showing the average conditions in a C17th household. 'The complete woman' shown performing her everyday chores has to cope with an open fire which allows the smoke to escape freely into the room.

2.2 Turk Farm (Cloth Hall), Smarden, Kent.
Example of smoke hole, at the gable apex (right).

An improvement in the smoke disposal of the central hearth was made by the introduction of the louvre (from the French *l'ouvert*). It consisted of an often hexagonal opening in the roof, from which a turret was raised, with side outlets for the smoke (see fig. 2.3, 1.13). The same system is still being used today for ventilating barns.

The wall fires used much more advanced methods due to the Normans' understanding of the flue and stack system. They developed the funnel-like tunnel, cut inside the wall, into flues that carried away the smoke from one or more fires, often one above the other, to tall, cylindrical stacks open at the top. For each fire, the flue often branched off into two separate shafts, built of small red bricks, each with its own stack (see fig. 1.3).

EARLY ENGLISH AND MEDIAEVAL PERIODS TO THE FIFTEENTH CENTURY

The smoke from a central hearth wood fire could be disposed of with the help of the louvre but, for the poor, this was a costly method, and for a long time they resorted to cheaper improvisations, such as 'the headless barrel'. This was mentioned as late as 1610 when Bishop Hall could still describe a cottage thus:

> 'Of one baye's breadths, God wot ! a silly cote
> Whose thatched sparres are furr'd with sluttish soot
> A whole inch thick, shining like black-moor's brows
> Through smok that down the head-les barrel blows.'[1]

The poorer the owner of the fire, the worse was his fuel and the more smoke it produced.

Rich owners of central hearth fires were using best quality wood— ash or even oak—which burned well even when green and hardly produced any smoke, especially if charcoaled first. Charcoal (or 'coal' as it was referred to) was an almost perfect fuel; it gave plenty of heat, little ash and no smoke or smell, but it consumed large quantities of wood. The 'Household Book' of the Duke of Clarence for 1469 showed that £106 9s. 4d. was paid in that year for 'wood and coale', an enormous sum for those times, giving us some idea of the huge amounts of wood required.

By the twelfth century the vast forests of England had steadily dwindled, and restrictions began to be enforced. The law was that 'if a man, standing on a half burried stump of an oak, or other tree, can see five other trees cut down about him that is regarded as waste'.[2] Royal foresters collected 'cheminage' for the wood cut along forest roads, and, whilst no commoner could fell a tree, he enjoyed rights of 'lop and top' in quantities he was able to carry on his back.

Peat was one alternative fuel in plentiful supply, but, while it burned readily, it made a lot of smoke and an unpleasant smell. Some burned turf or peaty soil or even dried cow dung, all producing unbearable amounts of smoke. Under these conditions, various measures were taken up to stop the smoke getting to every corner of the house. One long-standing method was the custom of having two

1 Cited in Lloyd, 1975, p. 93.
2 Wright, 1964, p. 63.

2.3 Old Manor House, Woodstock, Oxfordshire. Example of stone louvres.

2.4 Examples of mediaeval flue termination.

a Mediaeval stacks such as this one at Sully sûr Loire in France, were often crowned with iron caps which were meant to split up the force of the wind allowing the smoke to get away unhindered and, at the same time, provided a decorative feature.

b The moulded stone string projecting diagonally at the base of this stack at Château Sémur-en-Auxois, provided a gutter at the top and sides, collecting the rainwater and preventing it from running down the face and penetrating under the roof covering.

a   *b*

doors in the centre of each of the side walls, which would be judiciously opened according to the prevailing wind.

In some instances, narrow bays were provided to contain the smoke; in others 'smoke hoods', wood and plaster canopies or 'covers', supported by a timber frame (see fig. 1.11, 1.13). When later an upper storey was inserted in rooms originally open to the roof, the floor of the upper storey was often level with the 'mantel tree' or the canopy which covered the fire. It was in this way that the so-called 'room in the chimney', the subject of many a tale, was created.

Some of the construction methods were extremely efficient. For instance, the bay, constructed of oak timbers and clay 'pug', inserted in the middle of Marley Farmhouse (Smarden, Kent), although built in the sixteenth century using mediaeval techniques, was so successful that it was still in daily use in 1931, and no stain or smoke had yet penetrated it at any point.[3]

The wall fireplace, meanwhile, continued to employ the Norman flue and chimney-stack system. Mediaeval craftsmen took minute care in detailing to ensure a trouble-free performance for their chimneys, at the same time producing a wealth of beautiful decorations.

Chimneys were often crenellated or topped with sheet-iron caps which split up the force of the wind and allowed the smoke to escape more freely, (see fig. 2.4). The chimney caps had sloped tops to hinder rain falling down the flue, while the stacks were provided with gutters and weathering to prevent the water running down the face of the stack finding its way under the tiles. Chimneys were (as they still are) plastered or 'parged' internally to maintain a good draught, which could be hindered by air loss through even small cracks.

In the fourteenth century, the Earl of Richmond's hall in London was to have its walls plastered and also the 'tewels (tuyaux: flues) to the summit'.[4] The mediaeval formula used for 'parging' – cow hair and dung – has yet to be improved upon. The following mix was given by F.W. Macey in his 1899 specification:

Flue Lining =
1 part cow dung
4 parts hair mortar

Hair Mortar =
1 part lime +
3 part sand +
1lb clean, well beaten bullock's hair for each two cubic feet of lime.
(The same mix was used as an early mastic around windows.)

Despite its advantages, the cylindrical, open-at-the-top chimney introduced by the Normans was less used during the thirteenth and fourteenth centuries, when, either by association with the louvre or due to attempts to keep the rain out, many chimneys were being built with vertical openings at the sides like the one at Abingdon Abbey (see fig. 1.14).

---

3 Lloyd, 1975, p. 347.
4 Wood, 1981, p. 289.

2.5 Sir Hugh Platt's fire of 'cole balles'.

The transition to coal fires in the sixteenth century

Wood was becoming extremely scarce and its use for burning was declared by Elizabeth I 'as being a debasing of that which if nature did not at first intend, necessity must employ for better service'. The use of coal for the domestic hearth had to be accepted for obvious reasons as the Reverend Harrison pointed out in 1577:

'Of coal mines we have such plenty in the north and western part of our island as may suffice for all the realm of England; and so must they do hereafter, indeed, if wood be not better cherished than it is at this present.'[5]

'Sea-coal' was not a recent discovery (the term refers to its form of transport by coastal barge). It had been used for a long time for forges, kilns and other such small industries, but was unwelcome in the home. Its smoke was such a nuisance that, from as far back as 1273, coal use was forbidden in London, and later, Elizabeth I made it illegal while Parliament was sitting.

'Iron chimneys' (grates or raised baskets) were widely used, but as the old method of wood-smoke disposal (hole at the top or inverted funnel) often remained unchanged, the room would fill up with insupportable smoke, making coal fires in this period a sign of poverty.

From this time on, a long succession of 'smoke doctors', trying to find a way of curing the smoke problem, were to be associated with the open fire and to influence its construction. Among the first was Sir Hugh Platt, who saw a solution in the reduction of the size of the house's existing fireplace by means of a false back and sides, carried up just above the opening, thus contracting the 'throat' and improving the draught. He also considered the improvement of the fuel, and his book, *A New Cheape and Delicate Fire of Cole Balles*, published in 1594 suggested the use of a mixture of coal, loam and sawdust of oak, ash or fir which he claimed 'maketh a sweete and pleasing fier . . .' (see fig. 2.5).

However, the smoke from coal was still hard to tolerate, especially on an open hearth, and chimneys became a necessity. Many were built during this period, mostly of brick, replacing the central hearth. The Reverend Harrison deplored the change and saw it as a mistake:

'Now have we manie chimnies: and yet our tenderlings complaine of rheumes, catarhs and poses. Then we had none but reredosses; and our heads did never ache. For as the smoke in those daies was supposed to be sufficient hardening of the timber of the houses, so it was reputed a far better medicine to keep the good man and his familie from the quack or pose, wherewith as then verie few were oft acquainted.'[6]

As the wall fire recesses were deepened and walls not so thickly built, the chimney had to project either on the outside or the inside of the

5 Harrison, 1899.
6 Harrison, 1899.

wall, the external type being the earlier. In the transition from mediaeval practice, separate stacks were built for each flue, but towards the end of the century, as they became part of the general aesthetic design of the house, chimney stacks were grouped together. At first attached to each other in a solid block, they were later linked at the cap and base only, which enabled the wind to pass through them, thus eliminating the down-draught created by the wind hitting a solid block of masonry. Intricately decorated with moulded bricks at the beginning of the century, almost plain by its end, the chimneys produced by the sixteenth century were some of the most beautiful and distinctive of any age (see fig. 2.6).

2.6 Decorated brick chimneys characteristic of the sixteenth century.

Perfecting the coal fire

THE SEVENTEENTH CENTURY

Few must have shared the Reverend Harrison's enthusiasm for the benefits of smoke, for in the seventeenth century more and more people were striving to find an answer to the smoke problem.

The 'smoke doctors'
One fundamental principle was established during this period: as the column of air in the flue was heated, a dis-equilibrium between it and the colder and denser air outside would force cold air into the room, via the chimney (the only available access) in an effort to restore the balance, bringing some of the smoke with it. However, if the cold air was allowed into the room through a separate inlet (an opened door or window, for example), it smoothly drove the smoke up the flue, in a reverse process. This was to be the basic remedy of most 'smoke doctors'. Their 'smokeless' or 'smoke eating' fireplaces relied upon methods, some more ingenious than others, of introducing cold air into the room.

Louis Savot, a physician in Paris, who in 1624 was among the first to apply this principle, carried Sir Hugh Platt's ideas a stage further by reducing the size of the hearth and the height of the opening and tapering the flue to a much smaller area. Furthermore, to reduce heat loss, he introduced the 'convection fire' principle by fixing iron plates behind and at the sides of the fire, thus forming ducts through which the cold air fed in below the hearth was reintroduced into the room when heated, instead of being allowed to go to waste up the chimney.

Sir John Winter suggested, in 1658, a valve-controlled fresh air supply pipe under the hearth (see fig. 2.7), while Dalesme, in 1680, when presenting his 'Heating Machine' to the Royal Society, proposed an 'upside down' arrangement, whereby the fresh air entered from above, the smoke being extracted from below (see fig. 2.8).

Glauber prepared his famous salts using the 'Philosophical Furnace' he invented; the air in this case was introduced by an additional flue, instead of being drawn from the room.

In 1678 Prince Rupert designed and installed in his own chamber a prototype aimed at preventing the smoke from re-entering the room, rather than at driving it away with cold air. For this purpose, an iron baffle subdivided the space behind the fire, forcing the smoke to take a downward route before rising out. The upper half of the baffle was hinged to allow it to open for a better draw when the fire was being started and to be closed once it had got going (see fig. 2.9). To stop the smoke that came into the room as the fire started, an iron flap had to be added at the front. Later, Mr Bingham, a builder who constructed and advertised the Rupert prototype, replaced the flap with a 'fire cloth', which was to survive as an ornamental feature long after the opening had been reduced to modern proportions (see fig. 2.10).

An endless number of ideas came and went, little by little altering the construction and appearance of the fireplace. It was at this time that bends in flues started to be introduced as yet another way of cur-

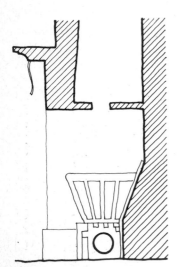

2.7 Sir John Winter's 'Fire Cage' project, which aimed to control the burning of coal with the aid of a cold air supply passing through the fire bed, met with a cautious reception from John Evelyn, who in 1656 remarked: 'What success it may have time will discover'. While it did not catch on at the time due to its difficulty in starting and burning performance, the same idea was employed in the development of combustion rate control in modern appliances.

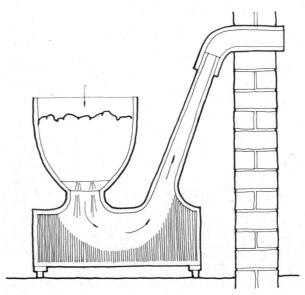

2.8 Dalesme's 'Heating Machine' (1680), one of the 'smoke consuming' fireplaces, was designed to create a downward draught fed into an 'upside down' fire bed (coal at the bottom, brush wood and kindling lit on top) assuming that the smoke of any added fuel would be absorbed through the air-suction effect of the burning coal.

ing down-draught, with some extremely curious shapes resulting (see fig. 2.11).

In one way or another, less smoke was coming into rooms, but, with the increase in the number of fireplaces, more and more coal fumes were released into the air, and this was a cause of concern.

In 1661 John Evelyn published an essay entitled *Fumifugium or the Inconvenience of the Aer and Smoak of London dissipated*, intended to draw the King's attention to the evils of sea-coal – 'the sole and only cause of those prodigious clouds of smoake, which so universally infest the Aer, and would in no City of Europe be permitted, where Men had either respect to Health or Ornament'. He suggested that 'workmen should be encouraged to make experiments, whether particular construction of the chimneys would not assist in conveying off the smoake' and as 'turning the noxious trades at once out of town may be thought impracticable' steps should be taken to 'oblige trades to carry their chimneys much higher in the air'.

The grate
Nevertheless, coal continued to be used on an increasingly large scale and was gradually accepted even in wealthy homes. This inevitably led to an improvement in the shape and construction of the fire bed container evolving from the iron basket and andirons to the 'Dog-grate' which combined the earlier components into one. In the eighteenth century this was further improved and simplified in the shape of the 'Hob grate' (see fig. 2.12). The fire was thus well raised over the hearth and fenders started to be used as protection against flying cinders.

THE EIGHTEENTH CENTURY

Experiments in the improvement of smoke disposal continued, and new prototypes appeared in increasing numbers.

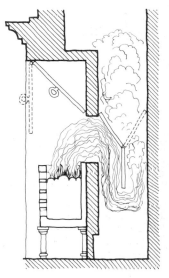

2.9 Prince Rupert's fireplace was fitted with a hinged iron baffle-plate and front flap, which were meant to control the air supply to the fire and encourage the issue of smoke up the flue.

2.10 'The Clergiman's Visit' by F.D. Hardy.
Evolved from Prince Rupert's iron flap, the mantel valance was to be found in the most humble of homes, as in this old country cottage depicted by F.D. Hardy. In wealthier houses the fireplace valance was to become an item of rather superior interior decoration. The 'Young Lady's Treasure Book' in 1880 was giving the following advice: 'Nothing is considered too costly a material upon which to paint or embroider a mantel valance, no pains ill-bestowed that serve to beautify these hangings, which are considered to constitute an elegant and highly acceptable bridal, Christmas or birthday gift.' (Cited in Lawrence Wright, 1964, p. 145).

2.11 A distorted flue terminal, one example in a long line of attempts to cure smoky fires.

2.12 The development of the grate.
a A first step towards the development of the modern grate was made in the C17th, as in this example at Penshurst Place, through the construction of the wrought-iron basket grate, which begins to render the andirons superfluous.

b 'Dog Grates' like this one at London's Charterhouse (1610) incorporated the still distinctive andirons or 'Fire Dogs' into the structure of the grate.

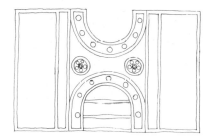

c The 'Hob Grate' consisted of a simplified metal front fixed into two brick boxes (hobs) built either side of a raised basket (top). The hobs helped to improve the performance of the fire by effectively reducing the opening, and, when at a later stage the brick was replaced by metal casings fitted with doors at the front, they doubled up as ovens.

At first constructed of one piece only, with a design strongly reminiscent of the andiron arrangement, the hob grate evolved into the 'double ogee' (centre) and the later 'duck's nest' shape (bottom), so familiar in late C18th fireplaces.

In 1714 Gauger devised a 'ventilating fireplace' which in effect was a combination of Savot's convection and Winter's controllable fresh air supply. Benjamin Franklin also tried his hand at finding a solution and introduced the 'smoke consuming grate' which employed Dalesme's idea of draught descending through the fire (see fig. 2.13). In 1745 he also attempted to improve Prince Rupert's descending flue in the Pennsylvania Fireplace (see fig. 2.14), and summed up his advice in *Observations on the Causes and Cures of Smoky Chimneys*.

Count Rumford's alterations to the fireplace opening
One important contribution was that of Count Rumford, who, in 1799, published an essay *Upon Fireplaces* which was to change a great number of English fireplaces. Adapted old grates were said to have been 'Rumfordized' and the man himself was declared 'the apostle of fireside comfort' and 'the fuel saver'. Rumford's approach was simple and effective:

'The whole mystery . . . of curing smoking chimneys is comprised in this simple direction: Find out and remove those local hindrances which forcibly prevent the smoke from following its natural tendency to go up the chimney. . . Reduce the fireplace and the throat of the chimney, or that part of it which lies immediately above the fireplace, to a proper form and just dimensions.'

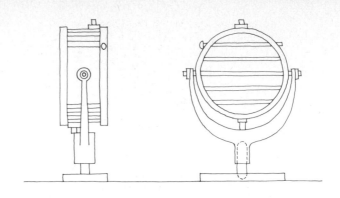

2.13 Franklin's 'Smoke Consuming Grate' (*c* 1785) employed a principle similar to Dalesme's 'upside down' fire bed, but instead of reversing the flame, Franklin reversed the grate by devising a revolving container which enabled the fresh fuel to be fed below the fire with the aid of a removable top bar.

2.14 The Pennsylvania Fireplace, devised by Franklin in 1745, used Prince Rupert's descending flue idea and Savot's convection principle. The cold air was introduced at low level and, having been directed below and behind the fire, re-entered the room warmed up, whilst the flow-back of smoke was impeded.
Left, elevation, *Right*, section.

Also to minimize the heat loss due to the heat absorption of the iron back, he recommended that brick or firestone should be used in lining a reduced and splayed recess (see fig. 2.15) The result was quite a success and, indeed, some complained of too much heat.

Rumford also revolutionized the kitchen with the introduction of his range which not only rationalized the use of fuel but greatly improved working conditions by reducing the heat.

Despite all the 'improvements' offered by inventors, the 'smoky chimney' was a continuing problem. From Reverend Woodforde's diary we learn that, in 1781, his study 'Chimney Place' was being altered for the fourth time. After six years a mason was raising and contracting both study and parlour chimneys but with not much success as, on one occasion when company was expected for dinner, both chimneys smoked at the same time. Although in 1794 both are yet again rebuilt, he is obliged to keep the cellar and study doors open and all the others shut, to drive away the smoke. In 1801 the study chimney still 'smoaked amazingly'. This must have been the story of many eighteenth-century households, and it is not surprising that many were becoming sceptical and concerned:

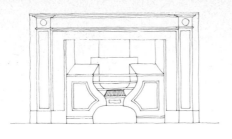

a

b

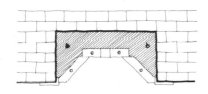

c

2.15 Count Rumford's fireplace
a The fireplace opening and hob-grate as used in Count Rumford's days.
b The same opening reduced by marble slips (a) and brick coving (c).
c Plan showing the alteration of the old opening with coving (c) and brickwork behind.

'To talk of architecture is but a joke
Till you can build a chimney that won't smoke.'[7]

and

'Architects and builders are still fallible in this respect, and often defeated by a rogue chimney.'[8]

and

'The builder of chimneys has been left to grope his way in the dark without assistance and in almost every instance his attempts to improve upon the practice of his predecessors have been unsuccessful.'[9]

As a result, many books were written on the subject and every builders' dictionary had some advice to offer. Of the better known, Richard Neve's *The City and Country Purchaser* (1703) and Peter Nicholson's *Practical Builder* (1797) gave precise dimensions and detailed instructions for the building of chimneys and the prevention of smoke.

Robert Clavering, a London builder who in 1779 wrote an *Essay on the Construction and Building of Chimneys* (see fig. 2.16) pointed out some of the problems of giving advice:

---

7 Cited in Wright, 1964, p. 101.
8 Cited in Eckstein, 1852.
9 Cited in Eckstein, 1852.

'Conceited Surveyors and Master Bricklayers are insulted by receiving directions; ignorant workmen become refractory if put out of old habits.'

The chimney pot

During the eighteenth century the clay chimney pot was introduced as a way of reducing down-draught, and although the idea has been attributed to Gauger's 'truncated pyramids' (see fig. 2.17), the principle was known in the middle ages. Despite the fact that it had no significant effect on the performance of the chimney, the patent clay pot has been associated with it ever since.

Nathaniel Lloyd saw the 'decadence of chimney design hastened by the invention of chimney pots', which, he felt, 'had attained ugliness scarcely surpassed by modern invention'. Nevertheless, chimney pots have become part of the English skyline, and their variety of design is fascinating (see fig. 2.18).

One final eighteenth-century feature related to the performance of the open fire was the chimney-sweep. The large chimneys of the old fires had been too big to clog up with soot and fairly easy to sweep, but the flues built or adapted for coal fires were much reduced in size, tortuous and impossible to clean with a brush or the old fashioned holly branch. The simplest and cheapest solution was to send up a small boy, and this practice was to make one of the oddest chapters in the history of inhumanity. By the end of the century a public outcry started, and in 1788 a Parliamentary Commission took evidence on the subject. However, it was only in 1875 that the use of chimney boys was finally abolished.

THE NINETEENTH CENTURY

Despite its advantages Count Rumford's solution was largely ignored by the Victorians, who preferred to use cast-iron fireplaces which were mass-produced by the foundries and much appreciated by builders for the minimal labour required in their installation.

Victorian inventors were not prepared to accept that Rumford had found the answer, and throughout the century there was a frenzy of patent fireplaces and accessories. Mr Peal's 'American Fireplace' had a movable mantel operated as a sash window, while Dr Backhoffner's was a double-decker grate with two types of coal, the one above intended to consume the smoke. Cutler's mechanical stoker fed coal by an elaborate system of cranks and chains, while the Dowson and Hawkins 'Patent Feeding Shovel' employed a box with a piston ejecting fuel onto the fire. The list goes on, and, by 1865, forty-eight such 'smokeless fire' patents were registered and many chimneys 'modernized'.

Meanwhile, the smoke was causing the world-famous London fogs, and, although, under the Public Health Act 1875, 'any fire not consuming its own smoke as far as practicable [was] to be deemed as a nuisance', no real progress was being made.

At the Smoke Abatement Exhibition of 1882 numerous appliances were tested, but none was successful in 'consuming the smoke'. Two years later, Dr Pridgin Teale introduced his 'Economiser', a box

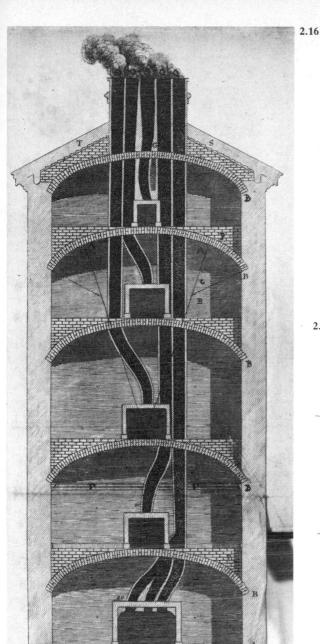

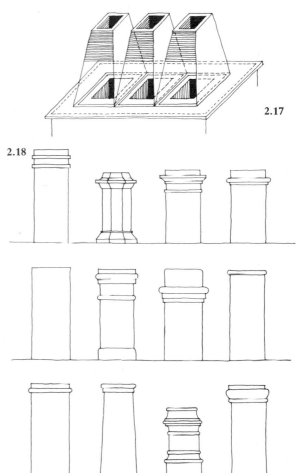

2.17 The C18th clay chimney pot is thought to have evolved from the 'truncated pyramids' devised by Monsieur Gauger in 1713 in an attempt to improve the draw of his 'Ventilating Fireplace'.

2.17

2.18

with an adjustable air shutter at the front which was formed under the grate. This simple device gave the answer and became an essential feature of the modern 'slow combustion' barless grate.

A breakthrough was also made in the perfection of the cast-iron kitchen range (see fig. 1.20b), although, as late as 1864, it was still quite normal in towns to send one's joint to the bakehouse. The closed stove, so popular in America, was fashionable for a while but it was never really adopted in England.

The use of gas and electricity as alternative fuels was beginning by the end of the nineteenth century but the gas or electric fire and range did not begin to compete seriously with solid fuel until the 1930s.

2.18 Clay chimney pots first became popular during George III's reign, but were not introduced on a truly large scale until Victorian days. Usually manufactured by local brickworks from tough clays, chimney pots were added to existing stacks in an attempt to improve draught by increasing the height. Pots could sometimes be as high as 2.3m.

The smokeless fuel fire and twentieth-century developments

The availability of alternative fuels and the Clean Air Act put an end to the search for 'smoke consuming' fireplaces. However, a way of constructing an efficient fireplace has been worked out and it is laid down in a British Standard Code of Practice (see p. 122 for further details). Flue liners ensure that the soot and fire risks are minimal, and the development of prefabricated chimneys now permits the installation of open fires in rooms that have no chimney. A far cry from the mediaeval smoke hole indeed, but the improvements of twentieth-century technology have brought about the loss of many unique examples of chimneys and fireplaces 'modernized' beyond recognition. Chimneys replaced by prefabricated ones and fireplaces blocked up and made redundant by modern heating systems have left many old buildings devoid of character and historically incomplete.

Development of features associated with fire risk

The open fire has always been a major source of fires in buildings, and throughout history there has been continuous concern over the methods and materials employed in its construction. The desire to reduce fire risks has influenced the development of the fireplace and chimney through a series of restrictive regulations affecting two main aspects: building materials and proximity to easily combustible elements.

From its earliest days, the clay hearth was mostly used in timber constructed buildings, and, while its central location was probably the safest from the point of view of the prevention of fire, the rush-covered floors and thatched roofs were easily set alight by flying sparks.

The Norman law of *couvre-feu* or curfew, passed in 1068 by William the Conquerer, was very likely intended to reduce the fire risk during the night when the hearth was unattended, by containing it with a metal or earthenware cover. It also helped to conserve the embers as a source for the next day's fire while, by fixing a time for these covers to be put on (eight in the evening), the Normans had a way of preventing nocturnal assemblies.[10]

Despite this law (which was abolished in 1100), fires increasingly devastated the towns which, like the City of London, were crowded with timber houses covered with straw. In 1088 Saint Paul's Cathedral was destroyed completely along with most of the city, and in 1136 it burnt again while being built.

We see the beginning of fire regulations in London from the first mayor's 'Assize of Buildings' of 1189 and the ensuing edicts of 'Wardmotes'. Along with party wall procedures and ancient light rights, directions were given to 'build stone houses covered with thick tiles to protect against the fury of flames and to avoid a similar peril'. 'Furnaces and Reredos' were not to be erected 'near laths, partitions or boards by which a fire might easily arise'.[11]

Scavengers (the mediaeval District Surveyors) were required to

---

10 Wood, 1981, p. 260.
11 Knowles and Pitt, 1972, p. 8.

swear an oath, undertaking, among other things, to oversee 'diligently' that 'chimneys, furnaces and reredoses are of stone and sufficiently defended against peril of fire'. Similarly, magistrates were empowered to enquire 'if there be any chimini that hath a reredos made uncomli, otherwise than it ought to be'.

However, hearths and 'flues' must have continued to be made of combustible materials because in 1419 the ordnance of the City of London declared that 'no chimney should thenceforth be made, unless it were of stone, tiles (ie bricks), or plaster and not of wood, under the pain of being pulled down'.[12] Similar fire prevention instructions were issued to parish councils and builders but they were largely ignored due to lack of pressure for their enforcement.

It was not until the great destruction caused by the 1666 Fire of London that fire prevention regulations began to be taken seriously. In 1667 Charles II passed 'An Act for rebuilding the City of London', which set strict rules regarding permitted building materials and methods of construction. Section XIVII referred specifically to timbers near chimney jambs, and forbade 'timber within the tunell of any chimney, with penalty and weekly penalty against workmen'. Within ten years London was a different city, and King Charles could say:

'Wee Found Our Citie of London of sticks and left it of brick being a material farre more durable safe from fire beautiful and magnificent.'[13]

During the eighteenth century the pace slackened as the memory of the fire faded, and further legislation became necessary. For example, a common way to clean up a chimney full of soot was to set it on fire. Problems also arose from the increase in careless building methods and poor quality materials employed by the rising numbers of profit-making speculative builders, whose mentality is characteristically indicated in the instructions left to his executors by one of the pioneers of jerry-building, Nicholas Barbon: 'to pay none of my debts'.

During Queen Anne's reign new Building Acts were passed, and further rules were laid down for the construction of chimneys and fireplaces, the Act of 1707 legislating 'for the better preventing mischiefs that may happen by fire'. Chimney jambs and backs were required to be nine inches in thickness with four-and-a-half-inch 'withes' (flue dividers), all funnels plastered or pargeted inside. Fires (in stoves or for boilers, etc) were to be built out with a permitted minimum distance from the adjoining building (nine inches) and timbers were not allowed to be closer than five inches to a fireplace or flue.

Later, in 1764, a clause in the Building Enactment laid down conditions regarding timber near or under hearths and chimneys, while party walls 'were not to be cut into or wounded for the purpose of making chimneys'.

---

12 Addy, 1905, p. 130.
13 Knowles and Pitt, 1972, p. 34.

Towards the end of the eighteenth century, much-altered chimneys were causing soot blockages in the flues, and the denser coal smoke was encouraging a rapid tar build-up which resulted in numerous chimney fires. Samuel Pepys experienced them and thought that firing a gun up the burning chimney was one of the best ways of putting the fire out. Parson Woodforde, in his diary, wrote about 'a very dreadful fire' in the chimney, which took two hours to control with water, wet rugs and blankets.

In 1834 a further act proceeded to improve this aspect by regulating the dimensions and shape of flues that would not only facilitate cleaning but put an end to the use of 'chimney boys': 'every chimney, being not a circular chimney of twelve inches diameter, shall be in every section fourteen inches by nine inches and no chimney flue shall be constructed with an angle therein, which shall be less obtuse than 120 degrees'.

Finally, the Building Act of 1844 was the first comprehensive building act for London and formed the basis for modern bye-laws and building regulations.

It is quite clear how modern fireplaces and chimneys have come to be built as they are, and why the building control rules contain the restrictions they do. But one would be hard pushed to apply these restrictions to fireplaces which belong to other times without altering them almost entirely. The requirements for standard fire back dimensions and tiled pre-cast surrounds make non-conforming old-fashioned ones – even Adam surrounds – easy plunder for the keen builder, while mandatory flue sizes and linings have been the cause of many demolished chimneys.

Summary of Historical Developments

Historical period	Architectural features		Smoke disposal		Fire risk
	Central hearth	Wall fireplace	Central hearth	Wall fireplace	
1 **Saxon**	Only central hearth used		Hole at the top		
2 **Norman** 1066–C12	Frontal firedogs for spits	Part of the structure		Flue scooped in wall with side outlets	Curfew 1189 'Assize of Buildings' gives regulations for building 'Furnaces and Reredoses' in London
3 **Early English – Mediaeval** C12–C15:	Timber structures Smoke bay	Stone structures C13 corbelled hood on joggled lintel	Louvre	Cylindrical flue and chimney shaft with top outlet	'Scavengers' (the mediaeval DS) on oath to ensure that fireplaces are safely built in London
Plantagenets 1154–1399 House of Lancaster 1399–1461 House of York 1461–1485	Smoke hood	C14 angle brackets C15 recessed pointed arches, height of Gothic			1419 City of London Ordnance requires hearths in London to be of incombustible materials
4 **Tudor period** Henry VII 1485–1509 Henry VIII 1509–1558 Elizabeth I 1558–1603	Floors are inserted in the hall Lateral iron dogs are used for supporting logs The kitchen is brought into the house. Brick and timber are used	 The Tudor arch is gradually replaced by a rectangular opening with ornametal decorations	Pargeted flues	Grouped flues, decorative brickwork chimneys Introduction of sea-coal. The first 'smoke doctors'. The size of opening begins to be reduced	General disregard of regulations, numerous fires

| Historical period | Architectural features | | Smoke disposal | | Fire risk |
	Central hearth	*Wall fireplace*	*Central hearth*	*Wall fireplace*	
Tudor period continued		Imported artists introduce the first elements of Renaissance			

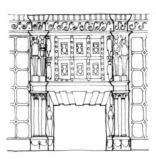

Iron dogs and fire bricks

Decorative brick work

| 5 **Seventeenth century** (Stuart period) 1603–1714 James I 1603–1625 Charles I 1625–1649 Common-wealth and Protectorate 1649–1660 Charles II 1660–1685 James II 1685–1689 William III and Mary 1689–1702 | Brick available widely

Sea-coal

The inglenook

Accessories (hooks, cranes, spits)

Iron chimneys | Classical design using marble, stone and plaster

Position in plan becomes subordinate to symmetry

Inigo Jones (1573–1723) the marble mantel shelf — full height design | | 1661 John Evelyn's *Fumifugium* 'Smoke-doctors' Savot Winter Dalesme Prince Rupert | 1666 Fire of London

1667 Charles II's Act for re-building London restricts proximity of combustible materials |

Summary of Historical Developments—*continued*

Historical period	Architectural features		Smoke disposal		Fire risk
	Central hearth	*Wall fireplace*	*Central hearth*	*Wall fireplace*	

Seventeenth century continued

Wren (1632–1723)
The over-mantel mirror and china shelves

The introduction of the hob grate (first only one front piece with bars)

---

6 **Eighteenth century**
Queen Anne 1702–1714
House of Hanover
George I 1714–1727
George II 1727–1760
George III and Regency 1760–1820

The demarcation between the central hearth and wall fireplace becomes less distinct

Pattern books and Palladianism: location in plan is dictated by symmetry at gables. Heavy bolection

Robert Adam (1728–1792) use of *scagliola* compo and soft woods with marble slip

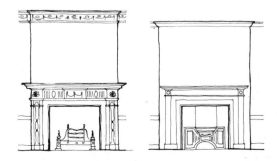

Count Rumford

Clay chimney pots

Chimney boys

1708 Queen Anne Act requires pargeting of flues in London

1764 'Building Enactment' Acts set further restrictions for the proximity of the hearth to combustible materials

Historical period	Architectural features		Smoke disposal		Fire risk
	Central hearth	*Wall fireplace*	*Central hearth*	*Wall fireplace*	
Eighteenth century continued	Neoclassicism: John Nash (1752–1835)				
	The beginning of the Gothic Revival: James Wyatt (1746–1813)				
	The hob grate increasingly made of two separate front plates (the ogee) or Adam gun steel baskets				
7 **Nineteenth century** House of Hanover The Regency 1811–1820 George IV 1820–1830 William IV 1830–1837 Queen Victoria 1837–1901	Mass-produced metal register grates and ceramic tile surrounds		Patents for smokeless or 'smoke-eating' fires Improvement in efficiency 1875 Public Health Act (abolition of chimney boys)		1834–1844 London Building Acts
	The kitchen range				
	Gothic revival: A.W.N. Pugin (1760–1832), John Ruskin (1819–1900), Sir George Gilbert Scott (1811–1878)				
	'Queen Anne Style' of Norman Shaw (1831–1912)				
	The beginning of the Arts and Crafts movement. Use of glazed brick				
	Charles Rennie Mackintosh (1868–1928)				
	Art Nouveau (1892–1905)				
8 **Twentieth century** House of Saxe Coburg	C.F.A. Voysey (1858–1941)		1936 Public Health Act		1930–1939 London Building Acts
	Sir Edwin Lutyens (1869–1944)		1956 Clean Air Act		1976 The Building Regulations
	Central heating		1968 Smokeless zones Smokeless fuel		
Edward VII 1901–1910	Town and County Planning Act				
George V 1910–1917					
House of Windsor from 1917					

Part II
Refurbishment and reinstatement of old fireplaces

The repair and maintenance of old buildings calls for an ability to understand and investigate old structures and building methods, for which a professional knowledge of building construction, such as that acquired by practicing architects and surveyors, is necessary. The following chapters are not specifically directed towards the small builder or DIY handyman and do not include basic or routine items familiar to the specialist. They do, however, provide general guidance to enable the layman to recognize the problems of fireplace and chimney construction so that he may seek the necessary professional advice in time to arrest the degradation of old building fabric. For those who do not have an established source of specialist advice, the following organizations may prove useful:

RIBA and RICS (Royal Institute of British Architects and Royal Institution of Chartered Surveyors)
have up-to-date records of practising architects and surveyors and can recommend one of their members who is currently undertaking small-scale refurbishment work or specializing in historic buildings.

The architect or surveyor will be able to advise on a contractor and supplier best suited for each individual case.

ICE and ISE (Institute of Chartered Engineers and Institute of Structural Engineers)
have up-to-date records of practising civil and structural engineers and can recommend one of their members who has experience in the relevant field.

The engineer will be able to advise on the structural aspects of the proposed work.

Local Authorities
The Building Control or Historic Buildings departments often have lists of approved contractors and can advise on the work involved if it is subject to statutory requirements.

SFAS (Solid Fuel Advisory Service)
have field inspectors, who, provided coal or smokeless fuel is the main fuel used, make site visits and give advice on each case. They can also suggest contractors and suppliers.

SPAB (Society for the Protection of Ancient Buildings)
will advise on listed/historic buildings and have lists of contractors and suppliers specializing in historic buildings.

The National Fireplace Council
has lists of suppliers, but is a manufacturers' association and cannot necessarily be expected to give impartial professional advice.

For further details on these sources, see Appendix II.

3
Problems concerning the building fabric

Chimneys and fireplaces are not only relevant to the character and history of old buildings: they also perform the beneficial function of ventilating rooms and the building fabric, aiding structural stability as well as providing a viable answer to the 'oil crisis'. It is therefore worth considering their re-instatement and/or refurbishment, and to be able to do this successfully, it is essential to be able to recognize common problems.

Due to their exposed position, chimneys are susceptible to damage by rain, wind and frost, while flue linings, already eroded by years of continuous use, can be badly affected by indiscriminate use of modern fuels and appliances. The size and shape of the opening has probably been altered beyond recognition by successive generations of 'smoke doctors', fire regulations and recurrent 'modernizations' of old houses. With careful maintenance and repair and thoughtful adaptation, the life of the fireplace and chimney can be lengthened and their benefits further enjoyed. For this purpose, the following notes may provide a practical checklist for dealing with the most common defects:

Defects leading to loss of structural stability

The structural stability of chimneys and fireplaces is most commonly affected by the following factors:

1 EROSION OF THE MASONRY THROUGH THE ACTION OF WIND, RAIN AND FROST (see fig. 3.1)

If the brick or stonework has been considerably affected, with more than a quarter of its thickness eroded away, the decayed sections should be carefully cut out and replaced with matching new materials (see fig. 3.2). The alternative of 'stone mortar' repairs on isolated stones should also be considered. Plastic stone repairs using impervious resin compounds, while being weather resistant in themselves, can in time become dislocated by moisture trapped in the porous fabric immediately behind the repair and unable to evaporate.

2 EROSION OF MORTAR BY THE ACTION OF WIND, RAIN AND FROST

This can weaken the chimney fabric generally and also induce a lean in the direction of the prevailing rain as the loss of gradually disinte-

3.1 Due to their exposed position, chimney stacks are often affected by damp, wind and frost, which can cause brick and mortar to deteriorate and gradually disintegrate.

grating mortar on the more weathered side leads to a settlement. The process is often accentuated by the action of frost on this, the usually damper side, where the mortar deteriorates through expansion. To prevent these defects, regular inspection and correct repointing of the joints, raked out to a depth of about twice the width, is necessary (see fig. 3.3, 3.4). The mortar should be brushed before it sets so as to expose the coarser aggregate.

3   EROSION OF MASONRY AND MORTAR BY THE CHEMICAL ACTION OF ACIDS FROM FLUE GASES ON THE INTERNAL WALLS

It should be remembered that many flues in old houses were constructed to carry away wood smoke and not the products of gas or solid fuel boilers, which often, when fed into unlined chimneys, cause a sulphate attack on the existing fabric.

Solid, gaseous and oil fuels contain hydrogen which, when combined with oxygen during combustion, produces water. This in turn combines with carbon or sulphur dioxide with the result that carbonic and sulphuric acids condense on the inner face of the chimney, attacking the mortar and gradually causing unsightly staining both externally and internally (see fig. 3.5), due to the penetration of sooty material carried through by excess water. Other symptoms of chemical attack can be:

a

b

c

d

e

3.2 Replacement of decayed bricks.

a   The surface of brickwork can crumble away gradually, and as a result the brick face flakes off and becomes recessed. This is usually due to frost action or to an excessive salt content in the brick which will be worse affected when underburned. Neglect can encourage vegetal growth which also contributes to brick dislocation. If only a few bricks are affected it will normally be sufficient to cut out and replace them.

b   The defective bricks should be carefully dislodged using a club hammer and cold chisel.

c   All broken and damaged bricks should be removed and the remaining space cleaned by brushing away the dust and loose mortar.

d   The cut-out spaces should be prepared by wetting and spreading mortar at the bottom of the hole. Defective bricks are to be replaced by new ones (whole or cut to size as the case may be), tapping them gently into place once 'buttered' (spread with a 10mm layer of mortar top and sides).

e   The work should be finished by pointing the new joints in a manner matching the existing, and when the mortar is almost dry, brushing lightly with a dusting brush to expose coarse aggregate.

- Cracking of the mortar joints
- Vertical splitting of the stack
- A bend of the stack
- Displacement of the chimney pots (see fig. 3.6).

If neglected, chemical attack can lead to a total weakening of the structure (see fig. 3.12).

Depending on the stage of erosion, the following remedies should be considered along with the eradication of the cause:

- Restore damaged masonry pointing (see fig. 3.3).

- If the damage is pronounced only above roof level, eroded flue dividers (withes) should be rebuilt, (see fig. 3.7).

- Restore the damaged existing lining. If, however, the use of modern fuels and appliances is intended, it is essential that the flue is suit-

3.3 Repointing.

a Rake out all loose matter using a metal hook raker made from a 150mm nail with one end hammered flat, or any other similar tool. (Using a hammer and chisel could result in cracked brickwork.)

b Brush away all dust and loose mortar, and soak with water the joints to be repointed. Mix the mortar to the same strength as the existing one, if this is not too hard and is in good condition.

c Press mortar into the brick joint until it is firmly packed and protruding slightly off the brick surface.

d Pointing.

1 Flush pointing
The joint is finished flush with the face of the brickwork. When the mortar is almost dry, rub with a piece of sacking, scrape off with a stiff piece of plastic and brush off dust.

2 Weathered pointing
The joint is sloped downwards to throw off rainwater. The surplus mortar is removed by trimming with the trowel against a straight feather-edged batten.

3 Keyed pointing
Known also as 'bucket handle' pointing, in this case the mortar is pressed into the joint with a rounded tool which can be an old bucket handle or a piece of hose pipe.

e When the mortar is almost dry, brush the surface lightly to expose the coarser aggregate.

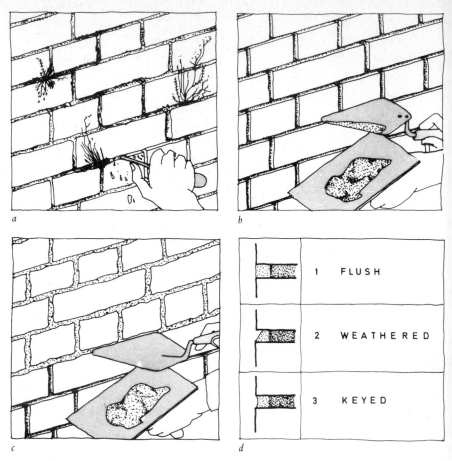

a

b

c

d

	1	FLUSH
	2	WEATHERED
	3	KEYED

e

ably lined to safeguard it from further damage and that the gap between the liner and the existing flue is filled up to prevent the build-up of condensation and for better insulation.

A detailed account of lining methods, materials available and their characteristics is given in chapter 6, pp. 114–117.

● If chemical erosion has been allowed to reach an advanced stage, it can disrupt the structure of the chimney to such an extent that it may have to be dismantled and rebuilt.

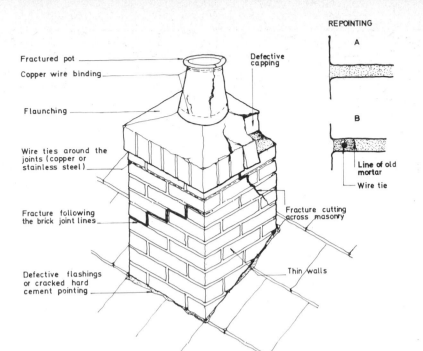

Fractured pot

Copper wire binding

Flaunching

Wire ties around the joints (copper or stainless steel)

Fracture following the brick joint lines

Defective flashings or cracked hard cement pointing

Defective capping

Fracture cutting across masonry

Thin walls

REPOINTING

A

B

Line of old mortar

Wire tie

3.4 Common defects affecting chimney stacks.

3.5 Condensing flue gases can cause chemical attack of the flue and characteristic brown staining.

3.6 Common symptoms of sulphate attack in the flue.

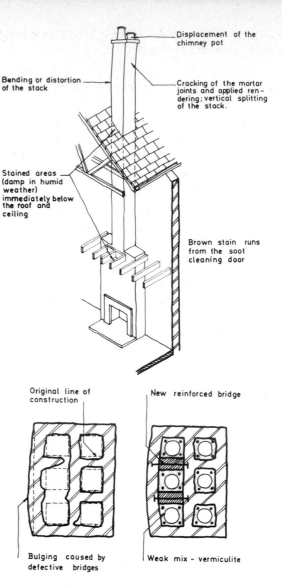

Displacement of the chimney pot

Bending or distortion of the stack

Cracking of the mortar joints and applied rendering; vertical splitting of the stack.

Stained areas (damp in humid weather) immediately below the roof and ceiling

Brown stain runs from the soot cleaning door

3.7 Deterioration and repair of flue dividers (withes).
Plan, left, showing faulty condition of the dividing bridges as a result of which the 'ties' are lost and the wall of the stack is bulging.
Plan, right, showing the extent of remedial work necessary to consolidate the chimney, consisting of:
● insertion of new withes constructed of reinforced concrete.
● consolidation of flue walls in situ with a reinforced weak mix of vermiculite and concrete.
● installation of new lining to suit the type of fuel used.

Original line of construction

New reinforced bridge

Bulging caused by defective bridges

Weak mix - vermiculite

4   FRACTURING OF MASONRY CAUSED BY SETTLEMENT, UNEQUAL LOADING OR FROST

Unequal loading caused by alterations or faulty design is associated with pressure of deflecting beams or angled eccentric thrusts, and can cause bulges and cracks. Similarly, frost can have a detrimental effect, especially if water has seeped into the masonry.

If the fractures follow the joints, (see fig. 3.4), and are not extensive, correct repointing is a sufficient remedy. If the fractures cut across individual stones or bricks, these should be replaced if the damage is isolated (see fig. 3.2). But, if the cracking is extensive, complete rebuilding may be required.

CAUSES OF LEAN ABOVE THE ROOF

1   As shown above, a lean above the roof can occur as a result of

weather damage or of chemical attack, present especially when slow combustion fuel appliances are used.

2   Another cause of leaning chimneys is the movement which may occur in old buildings due to:

● *Inadequate design*, such as insufficient thickness of walls. This, if there is no restraint, causes leaning. In the absence of horizontal restraint, such as internal flue dividers or floor structure, the flue walls will bulge and, if there is some vertical restraint at corners, horizontal bows will occur (see fig. 3.7).

● *Faulty construction* and/or materials, such as inadequate bonding, which can cause sections of brickwork to break away. This is usually a local effect and can be recognized by slight bulges and a hollow sound when tapped lightly.

● *Faulty or insufficient foundations* or change in the bearing capacity of the subsoil. Foundations can become inadequate as a result of overloading brought on by alteration, the introduction of new openings or the enlargement of old ones.

● *Roof thrust*, which can cause instability by transferring additional unequal loads. Structural ties should be introduced in this case.

When the cause of movement has been dealt with, the stack can either be jacked back into the vertical position (see fig. 3.8) or consolidated in situ as the case may be (see fig. 3.10, 3.11).

3   Thermal change can be another cause of leaning chimneys, especially where they stand very high above the roof. They often assume a permanent curvature which may be arrested with the correct lining.

4   Excessively high stacks where old stacks have been raised above their original levels in an effort to prevent down-draughts due to new neighbouring buildings or trees. These if of a flimsy construction, suffer a toppling movement. A commonly used remedy is the iron strap and stay, (see fig. 3.9) which, apart from being unsightly, provides mostly visual support. The chimney should be stabilized or, if research indicates a lower original height, reconstructed accordingly.

CAUSES OF LEAN BELOW THE ROOF

1   If the chimney lean appears below the roof and towards the fireplace, it probably represents shrinkage of the chimney beams. If there are two or three fireplaces one above the other, the existence of shrinkage may represent quite considerable loss of height on the face. The reasons for the shrinkage should be detected and dealt with and the chimney stabilized in situ if possible. Reasons can be:

● Newly installed central heating which can cause the drying of timber lintels.

Existing chimney leaning through loss of support due to decayed timber wall plate

Replace rotted ends of rafters and strengthen with new rafters spliced over. If there is an existing offset, additional support such as a concrete corbel should be provided.

Defective wall plate replaced by brickwork or concrete

Joints raked to allow for jacking movement

3.8 A leaning stack can be jacked back into a vertical position. A difficult and expensive technique, this is usually considered in the case of historic buildings and should not be undertaken without specialist advice.

In the example shown, the lean was caused by the loss of support due to the disintegration of a decayed wallplate. After raking the joints into the opposite side so as to form a hinge, the stack is jacked into the vertical whilst a new supporting plate is inserted to replace the defective one.

● The drying out of replacement timbers, insufficiently cured when installed.

● The weakening of the fabric of existing overmantel beams due to boring insects or fungal attack, which can cause it to become crushed under the vertical load of the masonry above.

2 Chimney cleaning with weighted brushes or heavy hanging chains, lowered from the top, can cause damage and cracks to the internal linings and walls. Adequately sized flue brush and brush handles are a much better method, as is the old-fashioned holly branch.

3 Attachments, such as television aerials, weather cocks, British Telecom or electricity cables can cause corrosion, movement and fractures to the stack (above or below the roof). If they cannot be repositioned, their effect should be inspected regularly.

REMEDIAL WORK FOR STABILIZATION OF CHIMNEY STRUCTURES

Extensive failure due to one or more of the causes listed above can lead, with neglect, to a danger of collapse, and total rebuilding may be the only solution. But this should only be undertaken after considering whether the chimney can be stabilized in one of the following ways:

3.9 Excessively high chimney stacks (often extended in an attempt to cure down-draught caused by taller neighbouring objects) can easily topple over and collapse through the roof. Iron stays are sometimes fitted to restrain this tendency but like the one shown in this example, they seldom offer real support.

1 Chimney stabilization in-situ for continued use

If the dimensions of the chimney permit it, a hollow-cored, reinforced concrete lining can be cast inside an existing chimney in-situ to give it additional structural support. This can be achieved by lowering a flue liner inside the stack and using it as shuttering for the concrete to be poured between it and the chimney wall. It is essential that the space between the new liner and the existing flue is at least 100mm to enable sufficient concrete to be cast around the reinforcement bars (see fig. 3.9), which is often possible in the case of mediaeval stacks which are usually quite large. This method has the advantage that, apart from consolidating the stack structurally, it allows a continued use of the fireplace for heating and ventilation.

2 Chimney stablization in-situ when use is to be discontinued

A method which gives a good structural support (especially to richly decorated brick shafts which would be damaged if dismantled), this has the disadvantage of making the use of the fireplace impossible as well as causing the loss of its ventilating function, which is so beneficial to the fabric of the building. The work consists of casting a reinforced concrete core which fills the stack completely. A thin,

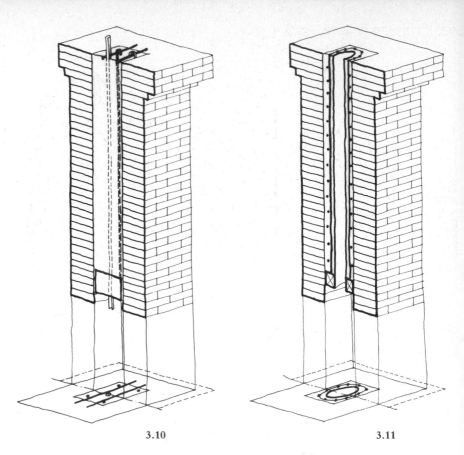

3.10 Stabilizing a chimney stack in-situ when the use is to be discontinued.

3.11 Stabilizing a chimney stack in-situ for continued use.

3.10   3.11

hollow pipe can be incorporated to encourage some air movement, but its effect will be fairly minimal (see fig. 3.10).

Both methods require careful consideration before implementation as they effect a virtually irreversible alteration, the removal of which, if required at a later stage, could prove impossible without some damage and dismantling of the original fabric.

3   Insertion of wire ties in joints before repointing (see fig. 3.4)
This method is applicable to smaller chimneys where commonly only the top section of the stack is in poor condition. The same method can be used for fractured pots. (If replacements are required, pots of the traditional design can be obtained from specialized suppliers. See Product Information Sheets 6, 10.)

4   Jacking back into the vertical position (see fig. 3.8)
This method requires experience and a good understanding of old buildings. It is suitable for special cases, when the historic fabric must be retained, but it should be undertaken only under specialist supervision. The joints on the side opposite the lean should be raked out to form a hinge, and the structure is then jacked into position and provided with suitable support before repointing.

An example illustrating almost all the types of decay discussed in this section is shown in fig. 3.12, where the chimneys of a row of

a   Before repair. (The top of the second chimney from the left has been badly affected by weather erosion, the third one shows a lean in the direction of the prevailing rain, accentuated by a sulphate attack curvature whilst the fourth has lost structural support on its left side.)

b   After the completion of refurbishment work. (By applying methods similar to those discussed here, the chimneys have been successfully reinstated.)

neglected cottages have reached various stages of structural instability. By applying the methods outlined earlier, they have now been reinstated successfully, as can be seen from the view of the same cottages after refurbishment. If, however, a building's neglect persists and the symptoms of instability are ignored, a progressive deterioration will occur, bringing the structure to the point of collapse, when irreversible damage can no longer be avoided (see fig. 3.13).

3.13 A continued neglect of structural problems will eventually lead to total collapse.

Damp penetration

The penetration of damp not only damages the chimney itself, but can also cause extensive damage to the roof and thus the whole building. Good maintenance and careful weathering details are in most cases the answer in preventing the destructive effects of damp.

Common causes of damp penetration and appropriate remedial work are:

I   LACK OF TOP PROTECTION (see fig. 3.4)

The absence of chimney capping and/or a defective flaunching will enable rain to come down the flue, straight onto the hearth below, affecting performance as well as saturating the stack walls through their unprotected top. Also the rain will be able to wash down the face of the stack wall and penetrate the roof at the junction line.

The design of chimney tops has been a carefully considered detail since mediaeval days, when functional features were also given a decorative value. The example shown in fig. 2.4 shows how stacks were provided with a projecting string which formed a gutter at the base of the stack and enabled the rain water to drain away at the sides of the base, thus avoiding penetration under the roof covering.

Defective capping and flaunching should be repaired or reinstated as necessary in accordance with the principles described in chapter 7, p. 123).

2   INADEQUATE THICKNESS OF THE FLUE WALLS

If the walls of the flue are too thin (for example, brickwork under 225mm thick), they will easily get saturated by rain water and become decayed. For this reason, and because of the often related structural instability, flue walls which are too thin should be lined, strengthened or re-built with a suitable thickness of wall.

3   DISUSE

When the use of a fireplace and chimney has ceased, the fire and hot gases no longer help to keep the chimney dry. A damp chimney will cause secondary dampness in other parts of the building through the absorption of damp by salts in the masonry elsewhere. To avoid this, disused chimneys should have suitable protection at the top and a maintained ventilation throughout helping to dry some of the damp. Possible ways of maintaining ventilation in a disused flue can be seen in fig. 3.14.

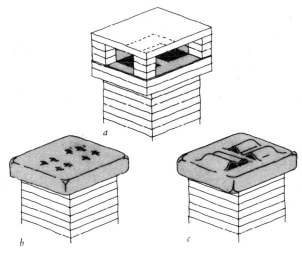

3.14 Maintaining ventilation in disused flues.
a   A common method of protecting the fabric of a chimney against the weather and at the same time of maintaining the use and/or ventilation effect of the flue, consists of the installation of a 50–75mm thick concrete, stone or clay slab at the top of the stack. This can be executed after the removal of the old pots and capping by placing the slab on 300mm high brick supports built at each corner on top of a lead or slate layer which will be necessary to protect the wall of the flue from being saturated with rain-water. Whilst this method will alter the general appearance of the stack, it has the advantage of being able to cure down-draught problems in certain cases.
b   When it is desirable to maintain the original appearance, lead sheet can be dressed over the top of a chimney or chimney pot and a certain amount of ventilation maintained by piercing small holes and lifting one side in an 'eyebrow' manner.
c   A more efficient ventilation can be provided by dressing the lead sheet over half-round tiles or pot sections bedded over the outlet of the flue.

4   DEFECTIVE OR ABSENT DAMP-PROOFING AT THE POINT WHERE THE CHIMNEY PENETRATES THE ROOF

This is a particularly dangerous situation, as the close proximity of the roof timbers and lack of ventilation will encourage dry rot in damp conditions. Chimney stacks should have carefully executed damp-proof courses both under the flaunched capping and at the base where they penetrate the roof.

● The material used should form a continuous impervious membrane properly lapped and flexible so that it is not destroyed by thermal or differential movement (see BS 743, 1970). Slates, engineering bricks or a layer of waterproof cement do not make suitable damp-proof courses, due to their inherent inflexibility.

● The damp-proof course must extend through the full thickness of the wall and project or be continued by a metal flashing as in fig. 3.15 and 7.4, to stop water running down the surface and seeping in below the level of the course.

3.15 Good protection at the point where a chimney intersects the roof is essential in avoiding damp penetration. It is accepted practice to achieve this with the aid of lead sheet flashings which can be cut and shaped to fit accurately any type of roof. The shaping of lead can be done by 'bossing' (the lead is beaten into shape) or 'leadburning' (the lead is welded). The usual components of lead protection around a chimney at roof level are:

The front apron, usually as long as the stack's width plus 150mm at either end for lap and about 350mm wide (150mm upstand and 200mm for cover down the roof slope). The apron is shaped to fit the roof pitch and often is part of a DPC tray which extends over the entire stack just below roof level (see also fig. 7.4).

The back gutter should be as long as the stack width with a minimum of 225mm at each end for shaping (more if the roof covering has deep contour single-lap tiles) and 475mm wide (100mm upstand, 150mm sole and 225mm lap up the slope, under the tiles). The back gutter is usually placed in position complete before the roof coverings are laid.

The side flashings are similar to ordinary abutment flashings and should have a minimum 100mm upstand, tucked at least 25mm into the brickwork joint and a 200mm lap under the roof tiles. *Cover flashings* are fitted at the corners to protect the brickwork at the ends of the side flashings and apron upstands. Smaller pieces of lead sheet (soakers) can be fitted as a cheaper substitute for stepped flashings, but due to the increased number of joints they can be less efficient.

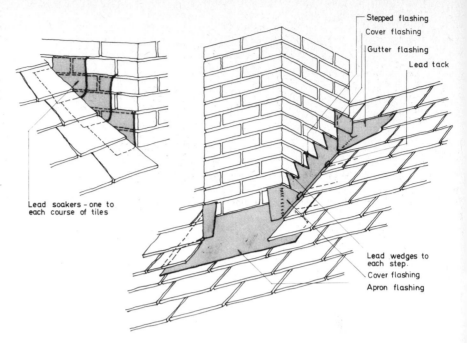

Lead soakers - one to each course of tiles

Stepped flashing
Cover flashing
Gutter flashing
Lead tack
Lead wedges to each step
Cover flashing
Apron flashing

When dealing with an existing building, especially in the case of historic features, it may be necessary to insert a DPC in-situ. An established technique employs the cutting of one or two courses of brick (or of a narrow slot in the bed joint) by hand or machine. The cuts should be made in short lengths (600mm or less depending on the wall loading) and the old brick replaced with dense engineering brick, slates or other DPC material. Rigid materials such as copper sheet can be driven in with the aid of a guiding frame (for further details see Ministry of Public Buildings and Works Advisory Leaflet No: 58, HMSO, 1970.)

● In many instances, it is difficult to insert a damp-proof course without rebuilding the chimney, and in these cases an injected chemical type combined with regular inspection may be the answer.

Traditionally, an overhang was created in the stack to protect the slates or tiles underneath. The joint was pointed in cement-lime mortar, and with regular maintenance repointing this was an acceptable weather-proof detail. However, mass produced, cheap cement, which is a strong mix, lacks the elasticity necessary to withstand the movement of the stack, and this combined with new, smoother machine-made bricks which offer only a limited key have adversely affected this technique. The modern method (introduced in about 1880, using metal 'soakers') provides more satisfactory protection. Lead flashing and soakers, correctly designed and installed, will ensure a maintenance-free, water-tight junction (see fig. 3.15).

If standard methods of detailing are not aesthetically acceptable in a historic building the 'invisible' use of lead soakers can be employed (see fig. 3.16).

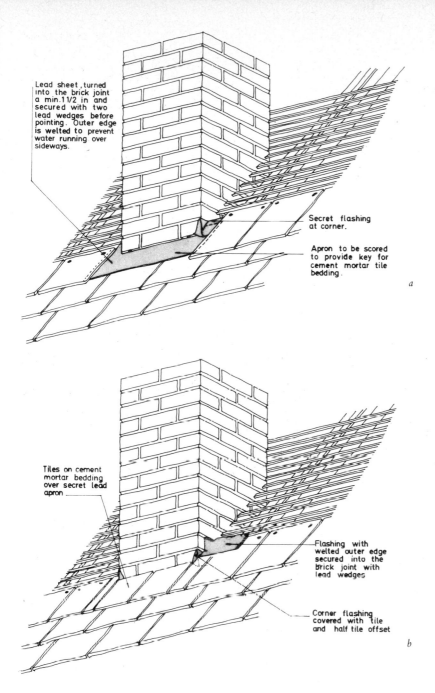

Lead sheet, turned into the brick joint a min. 1 1/2 in and secured with two lead wedges before pointing. Outer edge is welted to prevent water running over sideways.

Secret flashing at corner.

Apron to be scored to provide key for cement mortar tile bedding.

a

Tiles on cement mortar bedding over secret lead apron

Flashing with welted outer edge secured into the brick joint with lead wedges

Corner flashing covered with tile and half tile offset

b

3.16 'Invisible' lead soaker protection.
When it is wished to retain a traditional appearance, lead soakers can, if installed at the same time as the roof coverings, provide the necessary protection against damp penetration in an unobtrusive way. As this method will require a fairly extensive disruption of the roofing tiles it is best considered in association with re-roofing.
a The apron is placed in position at the same time as its corresponding tile course.
b Soakers are gradually dressed over the roof tiles.

5 CONDENSATION WITHIN A FLUE

This brings hygroscopic salts and tar to the surface, causing damp patches on the chimney breast, usually above the fireplace, both internally and externally. Redundant, blocked-up and unventilated flues are the cause of many damp patches in centrally heated houses.

Internally, in mild cases, the wall can be replastered and sealed with aluminium paint, applied once the plaster has dried out. But

c The roof tiles will eventually cover the apron completely.
d When the tiling is complete, the lead flashings are 'invisible'.

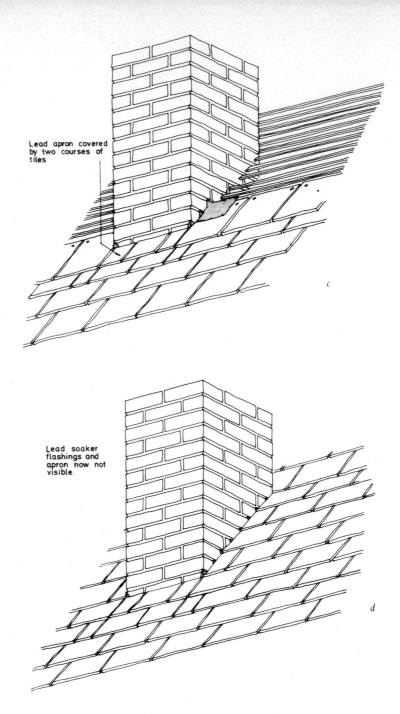

Lead apron covered by two courses of tiles

c

Lead soaker flashings and apron now not visible.

d

when the damage is extensive, the flue itself must be re-lined or at least the wall replastered or drylined in the affected area. If possible, this should be done with tanalized battens or 'Newtonite' lathing, (remembering to leave top and bottom ventilation gaps). Alternatively, a bituminous vertical membrane can be applied to the wall before re-plastering. It is essential, however, to maintain the flue's ventilation at top and bottom, (see fig. 3.14).

4
Problems concerning performance

While it is extremely difficult and, indeed, sometimes almost impossible to make old open fires comply with modern fire regulations, it would be foolish to ignore the fire risks associated with open fires. Each case must, of course, be judged on its own merits, but in some instances the risks can be minimized without necessarily defacing the appearance, so long as the likely causes are recognized and appropriate provisions made.

For this aspect in particular, there is much scope for improvement of building control legislation, which is structured to deal primarily with new buildings. Depending on the situation, however, relaxations can sometimes be obtained, due to an increased awareness of historical heritage values.

Causes of fires associated with the fireplace and chimney

The most common causes of fires are given below, with suggestions for prevention.

1 BUILD-UP OF CREOSOTE

Chimney fires can occur as a result of denser smoke, the condensing effect of cold flues and bad draught, which allows the smoke to be trapped in the flue. All these factors encourage the formation of a flammable deposit, creosote, a combination of soot and tar ($C_8H_{10}O_2$) which, if it has been allowed to build up, can easily be set alight by additional heat.

The build-up of creosote is encouraged by the following factors, which should be avoided:

- Lack of regular sweeping
- Bends in the flue, enabling pockets of soot to accumulate
- The use of fuel which produces a denser smoke, such as green wood, softwood or a combination of fresh wood and hot coal.

2 DEFECTIVE FLUE CONSTRUCTION

The pargeting or mortar rendering of a flue deteriorates with age, and in some cases such a rendering has never been provided. Cracks in the pargeting or liner joints can facilitate sparks and smoke penetration to adjoining timbers. A smoke test is a safe precaution if there is a doubt about the condition of the flue (see fig. 4.1). If serious leaks are found, the flue should be 'cored' or re-lined. (See chapter 6, p. 114 for details.)

4.1 The smoke test.
The purpose of a smoke test is to establish whether the flue is leaking through any cracks or holes, thus affecting the draw of the fire. The test consists of making a smoky fire (which can be made aromatic or coloured with a special powder additive obtainable from good ironmongers) in a fireplace which has been temporarily sealed with a dampened sack of wet straw or rags at the top and a suitable incombustible screen at each opening. If there are any leaks in the external wall or the internal dividers of the flue, smoke will be observed issuing in that area. Very slight leaks may be difficult to see, in which case a portable smoke detector alarm (like those used for children's rooms) could prove useful. This test can be dangerous and it is best carried out by a builder or a specialist engineer experienced in this type of work.

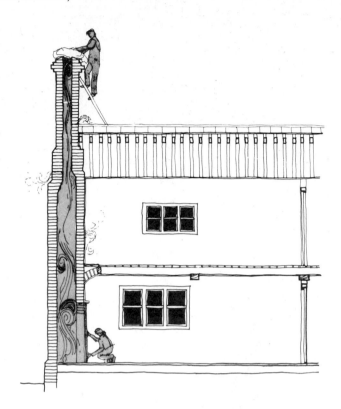

3 PROXIMITY TO COMBUSTIBLE MATERIALS

Often fires start as a result of insufficient separation between the fireplace and adjacent combustible materials such as floor and roof timbers. A hearth which is too small or cracked will allow sparks and hot cinders to fall onto floor boards or joists (see fig. 4.2a) and so cause a fire.

The risk is increased where a new floor has been laid over the old one and the hearth is in a sunken position, (see fig. 4.2b). The remedy, unfortunately, often involves either a new hearth or extensive re-building, which should not be attempted without specialist advice, as quite often it may involve structural alterations (see the refurbished stages in fig. 4.2).

Another example of fire risk is that of a defective or unswept chimney which will not only be prone to catching fire itself, but could also permit sparks to escape through cracks and endanger the roof timbers. The lining and structure should therefore be regularly checked for cracks and repaired as necessary.

Problems of smoking

This is one of the most common defects of open fires and, as has been shown, an important factor in their evolution. Many old chimneys

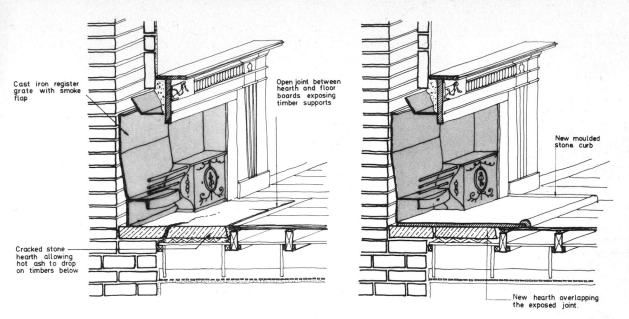

Cast iron register grate with smoke flap

Open joint between hearth and floor boards exposing timber supports

Cracked stone hearth allowing hot ash to drop on timbers below

New moulded stone curb

New hearth overlapping the exposed joint.

are now being used for smokeless fuel domestic boilers as well as for wood-burning stoves or open fires, and the problems discussed below apply to these alternatives too. Especially with modern demands for comfort, smoking is the most frequent reason for making alterations. Loss of historic features so often follows (as examined in chapter 2), and this should always be considered before deciding upon the extent of alteration work (see also chapter 6, p. 117).

A detailed account of the factors which affect the disposal of smoke from an open fire is given in chapters 6 and 7, where the main principles of operation and design are analysed. Here discussion is restricted to practical ways of recognizing and remedying defects associated with smoking.

Causes and symptoms of smoking fires

If there is insufficient draught to carry away all the smoke some smoke escapes into the room regardless of the weather or wind direction. Causes and remedies are as follows:

I INSUFFICIENT DRAUGHT

● *Air starvation*

This can be tested by opening a door or window. If the smoking stops, air starvation is the cause. The draw of the flue can be checked with a water manometer or by improvising a simple torch, such as a rolled up newspaper lit at one end, held at the bottom of the flue. If there is a good 'pull' the smoke will go straight up the flue; if not, it will float low and drift into the room.

To remedy this problem the volume of air going up the flue can be reduced by restriction of the throat as shown in fig. 4.3. Another method is to provide additional ventilation with the aid of grilles, ventilators or air inlets in the fireplace floor or walls (see fig. 4.5). If

4.2 Fire risk due to proximity of combustible materials.
a before (left) The floor timbers, hearth support trimmers and the ceiling below can be in danger of catching fire as a result of hot ashes and embers falling through cracks in the hearth or wide joints around it.

after (right) A new incombustible hearth (stone or concrete slab) should be laid to cover all cracks and overlap any joints between the hearth and the floorboards, thus protecting the timbers below. A moulded curb of similar material should also be installed to enclose the hearth.

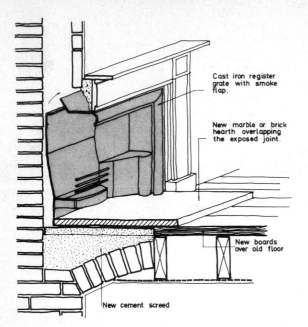

Cast iron register grate with smoke flap.

New marble or brick hearth overlapping the exposed joint.

New boards over old floor

New cement screed

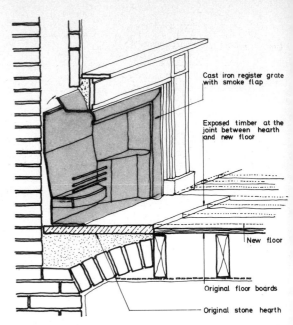

Cast iron register grate with smoke flap

Exposed timber at the joint between hearth and new floor

New floor

Original floor boards

Original stone hearth

b before (left) The timber floorboards and supports can be at risk when the hearth is level with or below the floorboards. This is often the case when a new floor has been laid over an old one.

after (right) The situation can be remedied by raising the level of the hearth, which can easily be achieved by superimposing a new incombustible hearth as shown.

this is not possible, a one-way grille can be installed at high level in an opposite wall (see Product Information Sheet 7).

The addition of grilles is a method particularly suitable in the case of large fireplaces, characteristic of the middle ages.

● *Size and shape of opening*

The fireplace opening (framed by the surround) can be too high or too large. To test this reduce the size of the opening by placing a piece of cardboard across the top and down the sides of the opening. If smoking ceases, it is too large.

To remedy the problem a permanent canopy or plate should be installed in the position proved most effective by the temporary masking. A toughened glass strip can be very effective while minimizing the visual alteration, (see fig. 4.6). Alternatively, the fault can be cured by raising the hearth (see fig. 4.8) and installing a hood, which can be made of metal (fig. 4.7), brick on a metal frame (fig. 4.11) or brick on brick piers (fig. 4.12). The alteration of the size and shape of the opening has been one of the most common modifications associated with fireplaces.

If a smaller opening has been or must be provided by infilling the original one, a record should be kept of the earlier arrangement. One quite ingenious way of doing this is shown in fig. 4.9, where sliding panels can be opened to reveal an earlier construction. Often however, the original work has disappeared unrecorded under later alterations. Sometimes, careful examination may reveal that what appeared to be a small Victorian fireplace hides a much earlier inglenook, more in keeping with the rest of the house (see fig. 4.10).

● *The size of the flue does not relate to the size of the opening*

The size of the flue must relate to the size of the fireplace opening. A recommended ratio is 1:8 (where the area of the flue is one eighth of the area of the opening), but the ideal proportion will vary from case

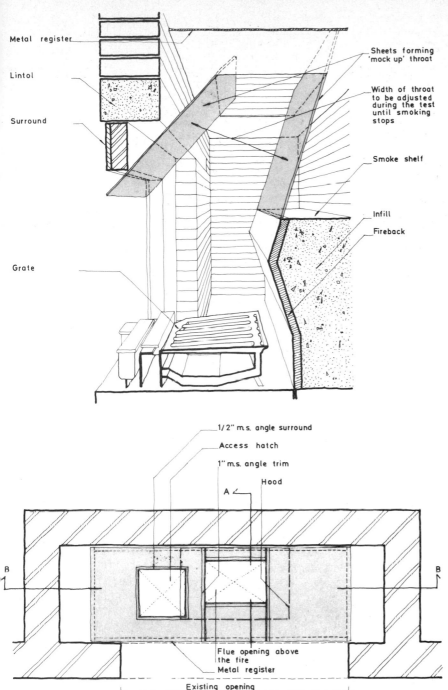

Metal register

Lintol

Surround

Grate

Sheets forming 'mock up' throat

Width of throat to be adjusted during the test until smoking stops

Smoke shelf

Infill

Fireback

1/2" m.s. angle surround

Access hatch

1" m.s. angle trim

Hood

A

B ──────── B

Flue opening above the fire

Metal register

Existing opening

A

a

4.3 Adjustment of the throat and gather of a flue to cure air starvation.

When there is insufficient draught due to air starvation, it is possible to remedy the fault by either increasing the volume of air coming into the room or reducing the flow up the chimney, thus decreasing the air demand.

Old fireplaces often have large voids at the point of transition between the top of the fire recess and the much narrower flue. The various nooks and crannies at the sides or the old smoke-shelf at the back (a surviving feature from Rumford's alterations) will hinder the flow by friction, encouraging smoke eddies. When the throat is not too large, a simple test can be made with the help of a 'mock-up' throat restrictor constructed of ply, tin or other fairly incombustible material. If by trial and error the 'pull' of the fire improves, the voids, shelf and corners should be filled in as shown, with a taper to allow a smooth air flow. The throat usually ends up reduced to about 100–115mm width. If the throat is very large a metal register (see fig. 4.4) or a proprietary throat restrictor (see fig. 7.3) should be installed under specialist supervision.

4.4 The insertion of a metal register.

a plan.

to case depending on the specific conditions (see chapter 7 for further details).

When, for aesthetic reasons, it is unacceptable to alter the size of the opening it is possible to modify the flue dimensions.

This can be achieved by inserting a metal register and/or a new liner.

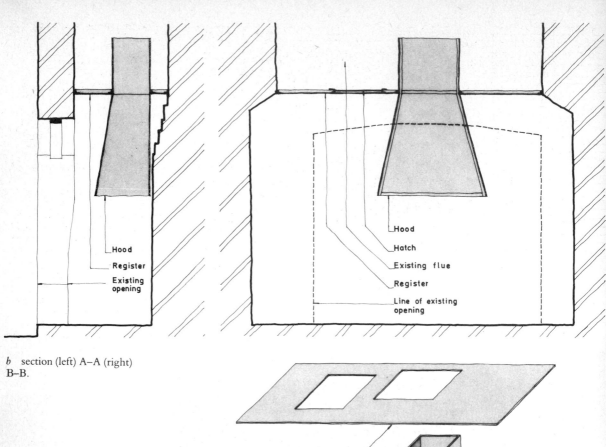

b section (left) A–A (right)
B–B.

c components.
This is often the best way of
adjusting the throat of a very
large flue such as those of many
ingle-nooks.
A metal register can be ordered
from any local metal sheet
merchant, who as a rule will also
be able to install it; but as the
design and fixing details can vary
considerably from case to case,
the advice of a specialist will be
required.

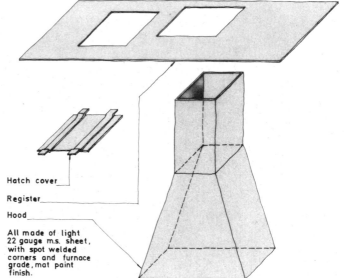

Hatch cover

Register

Hood

All made of light
22 gauge m.s. sheet,
with spot welded
corners and furnace
grade, mat paint
finish.

c

● *The shape and condition of the flue*
A flue can become partially blocked or have an unsuitable shape.
Most flues are off-set, either to by-pass another hearth in buildings
with more than one fireplace, or so constructed in an attempt to prevent down-draught. When the shape of the off-set has no regard for
the smooth air flow and, for example, has sharp bends or off-sets
which are too long or too low (see fig. 4.13) the draw will be hindered and the smoke will go back into the room. Also, if off-sets are
too shallow they can easily become blocked by soot accumulation or
mortar dropped down the chimney during construction or repair
work (see fig. 4.13).

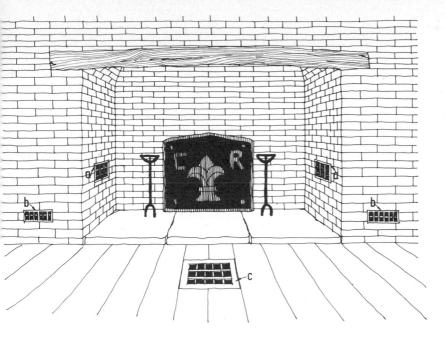

4.5 Improving up-draught in large flues.
Flues of old fireplaces are often large and require a strong up-draught in order to burn without any smoke drifting into the room. In the past, in houses with loosely fitted joinery and draughty rooms, most of the air needed was freely available, but modern comforts and sealed doors and windows make it necessary to introduce additional air by other means. One established practice is to install grilles or air bricks in strategic positions (either at the sides of the recess (a), or by the jambs (b) or, if there is a raised floor or cellar, in the floor at the front of the hearth (c), (see also fig. 4.6). If there is no direct access to an external wall, a high-level, one-way grille can be fitted in a wall opposite the fire, so as to draw air from an adjacent room, preferably the hall (see Product Information Sheet 7.)

4.6 Reducing the size of the opening.
A toughened glass plate strip can be an effective way of reducing a fireplace opening without significantly altering its appearance. (Note the draught flap in the floor which can be adjusted as necessary to increase or reduce the air supply.)

The test for this problem is by inspection with rods or sweep's brushes which may make it possible to assess the shape, position and approximate dimension of the off-sets and locate the blockage. The remedy, depending on the circumstances of each case, can vary from a simple chimney clean to the rebuilding of the off-set.

● *Size and shape of throat*
The throat may be too large or badly formed. The test is to fix a piece of cardboard or other sheet material restricting the throat as

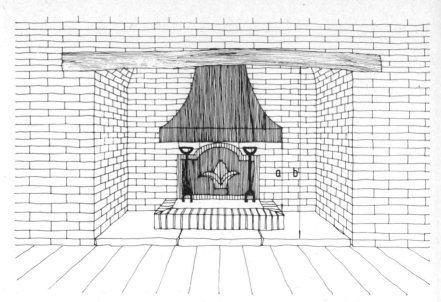

4.7 A common way of reducing the fireplace opening (from (b) to (a)) is to install a metal hood and raise the level of the hearth.

4.8 Example of raised hearth.

shown in fig. 4.3. If the smoking stops, the existing throat is not suitable, and it should either be altered or replaced by a proprietary throat restrictor.

● *Defective lining*

If the lining is defective it will allow air leaks which will interfere with the draw. A smoke test should be made to establish whether there is a leak (see fig. 4.1), and obstructions can be looked for with the aid of a sweeping brush or rod.

The remedy is to repair or replace the lining (see chapter 6 for details). Small or temporary repairs can be improvised by using a

4.9 Wall panels can be
constructed to slide open and
reveal the earlier
construction.

mobile coring plate which when pulled will press a lining compound
into the cracks (see fig. 4.14). A certain skill is required to maintain a
reasonably smooth liner surface and to recognize the best mix consistency.

See chapters 6 and 7 for further details concerning new liners.

● *Unsuitable or blocked chimney pots*
Inspection will reveal any problems; pots are not usually the sole
reason for the trouble, although they can contribute to it. The
remedy is refurbishment or replacement with suitable alternatives
(see Product Information Sheets 6, 10).

4.10 Original features can disappear without trace behind later alterations if they are not recorded, as in this example where there were no signs of the earlier ingle-nook until it was discovered by chance during the redecoration of a country cottage.

a   The fireplace before work began.
b   During alterations.
c   The fireplace restored to its original shape.

a

b

c

86

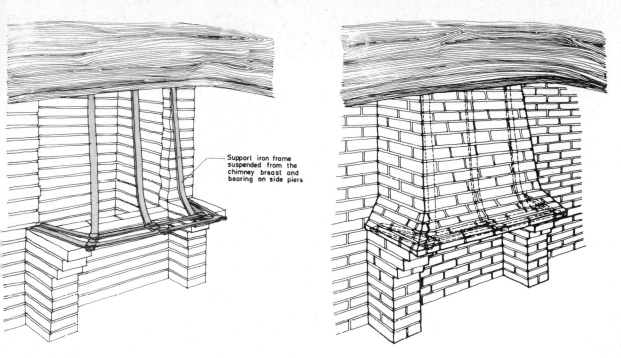

Support iron frame suspended from the chimney breast and bearing on side piers

4.11 A brick hood (right) which will pleasantly blend into the fireback background can be built on a supporting iron frame (left) suspended from the chimney breast.

4.12 A brick chimney and hood constructed on brick piers were skilfully inserted in the existing structure to provide a new fireplace for this converted barn.

4.13 The shape and condition of the flue offsets can adversely affect the performance of the fire when they are too shallow, too long or too low. Also, the bend can become partially blocked by soot, mortar or debris dropped from above.

4.14 A temporary repair to the lining of a flue can be made with the aid of a coring plate which can be improvised from a piece of blockboard, cut to fit the flue dimensions as closely as possible and weighted down with an object heavy enough to give it a 'pull', such as a brick or stone. After it has been wrapped tightly and connected top and bottom to a piece of strong rope longer than the chimney's entire height, the board can be pulled from the top of the stack gradually causing it to press excess mortar (poured in sufficient quantity from above) into the bigger cracks and holes of the flue liner. This is not an operation easy to execute and much depends on the consistency of the mortar which has to be just right – too thin and it will dribble at the sides, too thick and it will not allow itself to be pressed in.

As it can often lead to fairly disappointing results, this method is worth considering only as an emergency temporary measure.

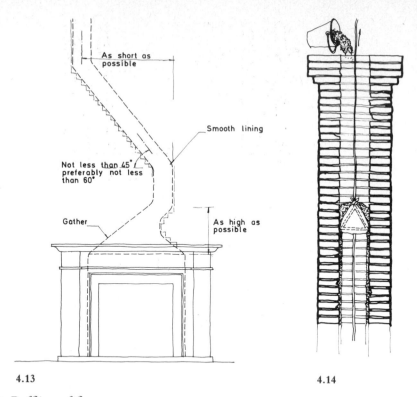

As short as possible

Smooth lining

Not less than 45° preferably not less than 60°

Gather

As high as possible

4.13   4.14

● *Baffling of flue gases*
The baffling or hindering of flue gases occurs when their smooth flow is prevented by an obstacle. This is common when modern closed or semi-closed appliances are fitted in the fireplace. The test is by inspection: usually the flue pipe will be found to terminate too close to the existing walls.

The remedy is to extend the flue. This also avoids the release of hot gases into a cold volume of air which will encourage poor draught (see fig. 4.15).

● *Air leaks due to faulty joints*
Draught can be affected by the cooling effect of cold air leaking into the flue through gaps around the register plates and the flue pipe joints or through cracks in the flue liner or brickwork. A test can be made by holding a candle inside the flue in these positions observing if the flame is drawn inwards, in which case cold air is leaking in. If access is a problem, a periscope or smoke test may be practical alternatives.

The remedy is to make good all faulty joints with special cement or with asbestos rope tightly packed into the gaps as a sealant.

NB Too much draught can also cause problems, especially with modern appliances, as too large a supply of air will affect their rate of combustion, speeding it up and causing the fire to burn brightly thus consuming the fuel faster than the efficient slow burning rate. Sometimes an adjustable draught stabilizer (effectively a flap which can open to varying degrees) will be required to be fitted close to the outlet of the flue.

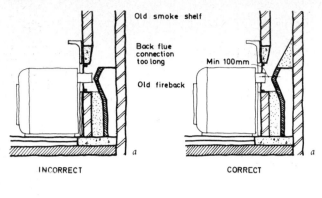

Old smoke shelf

Back flue
connection
too long

Min 100mm

Old fireback

INCORRECT   CORRECT

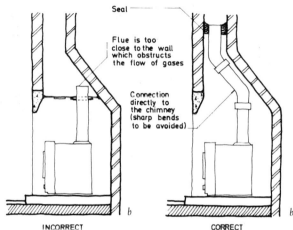

Seal

Flue is too
close to the wall
which obstructs
the flow of gases

Connection
directly to
the chimney
(sharp bends
to be avoided)

INCORRECT   CORRECT

4.15 The baffling of flue gases.
When flue pipes of free-standing appliances are terminated too close to an existing fireback or flue gather, the smooth flow of gases will be impeded, and as a result smoke will be released into the room by a semi-open heater, or in the case of a closed one the performance will be affected. Free-standing room-heaters should be so positioned that their back flue pipe has a clearance of at least 100mm (see *correct* 'a') or, in the case of a top pipe, this is sealed directly into the chimney, avoiding bends which are sharper than 120° (see *correct* 'b').

2   NO UP-DRAUGHT

In this case no smoke goes up the chimney, regardless of wind conditions. The causes and remedies are as follows:

● *Physical blockage*
The smoking will be constant and will fill the room regardless of wind direction or opened windows and doors, (see fig. 4.16). A sweep's brush meeting with resistance to its passage will indicate a physical blockage (bird's nest or broken pot pieces and other debris). If this has occurred the chimney must be swept and a suitable protection provided at the top to avoid recurrence (for example, the installation of a wire mesh).

● *Cold flue*
Fireplaces, especially if they have a large flue, will smoke when the fire is first lit, as it will take a certain amount of time to heat up the air in the flue and start the draught. The remedy is to warm up the flue before lighting the fire, using an independent appliance.

3   DOWN-DRAUGHT

A down-draught will blow smoke back into the room, steadily or intermittently, according to the direction and strength of the wind.

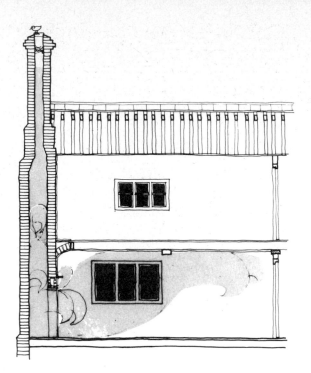

4.16 A physical blockage in a flue (such as a bird's nest or broken pot fragments lodged in) will cause a constant flow of smoke into the room regardless of wind condition or the opening of windows or doors.

This has been a problem throughout history and the tops of chimneys have been provided with countless preventive features, from Norman crenellations and iron sheetcaps to modern patent cowls (see fig. 1.7, 2.4, 4.17).

- *High pressure wind effect*
When a chimney top is in a high pressure region (on the side of the wind direction, see fig. 4.18), the fireplace will smoke, but only when the wind blows from a particular direction. To test this, open the windows on the side the wind is coming from (ie, the pressure sides). If the up-draught is restored and the smoking stops, the high pressure effect of the wind is causing the fault. If possible the chimney should be raised above the region of high pressure (above the ridge, for example). If not possible, one of the modern aerodynamic chimney cowls (see Product Information Sheet 6) should be fitted.

- *Low pressure wind effect*
Air inlets (doors, windows, etc) in a low pressure region (on the side the wind is going to) will draw the smoke by suction as a result of the difference in relative pressure. This defect is common with flues that are too short.

A smoke test (see fig. 4.1) will show that the smoke from the chimney is drawn towards the down-wind inlets. This is easier to detect if aromatic or colour additives are used. The remedy is to install a draught-inducing cowl on top of the chimney to increase the up-draught. This type of cowl (see Product Information Sheet 6) is constructed in a shape which, in conditions of strong wind pressure, induces a suction effect which helps create a stronger up-draught. A

90

4.17 'The Climax' universal ventilator advertized in the 'Ironmonger' of 1878 is one of many examples of Victorian patents promising a cure for smoky chimneys.

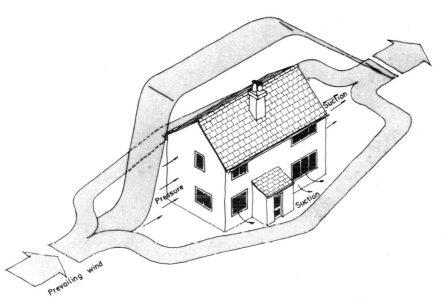

4.18 High- and low-pressure zones. Wind will cause air to flow around obstacles such as a house, creating zones of high and low pressure. In cases when doors and windows are located solely or predominantly in a low-pressure zone, the draw of the flue can be exceeded by the suction effect and smoke will be aspired into the room. Alternatively, if the outlet of the flue is in a high-pressure zone the smoke will be pushed back into the flue.

throat restrictor can also help by reducing the air flow and facilitating an increase in the temperature in the flue.

● *Neighbouring tall buildings and trees*
Air movement can be striking downwards because of higher adjoining buildings or trees which, in most cases, were not there when the chimney was built (see fig. 4.19). Observe whether the smoke is blown downwards as it tries to come out of the top of the flue. If so, modify the top of the chimney with a suitable cowl or a raised horizontal slab (see fig. 3.14).

Several efficient new chimney cowls are now available. One example, known as the 'Aerocowl' (see Product Information Sheet 6) was

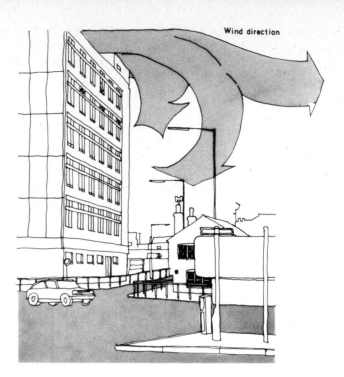

Wind direction

4.19 Downward pressure.
Neighbouring taller buildings or
trees can cause a downward
pressure when the wind blows,
and as a result, intermittent puffs
of smoke will blow into the
room. If, as in this example, it is
not possible to extend the top of
the chimney outside the pressure
zone, the top of the outlet must
be protected with a slab (see fig.
3.14) or fitted with a cowl (see
Product Information Sheet 6).

independently tested by the Northern Ireland Polytechnic Innova-
tion and Resource Centre and its satisfactory performance demons-
trated on the television programme 'Tomorrow's World'. Its
construction and design not only eliminate down-draught, but also
provide good ventilation to ensure minimum condensation and a
control of flue pressure, which can be useful with appliances which
require a balanced flue.

Conversion of existing fireplaces – summary checklist

When considering the conversion of an existing fireplace and chimney, a detailed examination is required to establish what refurbishment and adaptation work will be necessary. The survey should
cover the following points:

1   Structural soundness   The flue must be examined closely for any
signs of structural defects such as decaying masonry, a leaning stack,
cracks etc. (See chapter 3 for details.)

2   General condition   A check on the general condition of the flue
and fireplace should be made to locate such faults as chemical attack,
damp penetration, tar build-up, loose cappings etc.

3   General performance   A check for functional defects such as
smoking, air leakage, fire risks must be made. (See chapter 3,
pp. 77 and 78 for details.)

4   Heat source selection   The selection must be made from a range
limited by the fuel intended to be used and by the existing conditions, (size and construction of opening, structural support, etc). The

choice will then determine the extent of adaptation work necessary to provide suitable conditions for the use of that particular preferred source, indicating what type of liner, if any, is required, what additional structural provisions are needed, etc. (See chapters 5 and 6 for details.)

5 *Installation* It must be ensured that the proposed alterations comply with the appropriate statutory requirements. (See Appendix I for detailed checklist.) The installation must proceed in accordance with the manufacturer's recommendations and specialist advice must be sought for any variations which may be necessary because of existing conditions. (See chapter 6 for general installation guide.)

Part III
Modern fuel
and appliances

5
Modern fuels

As far as modern fireplaces are concerned, it is of course simpler if one can start from scratch. One can then cater for all the special requirements and preferences of a particular case, learn from past mistakes and at the same time satisfy modern requirements of construction and fire safety, which are, after all, intended for our protection. (The general design parameters and statutory control requirements associated with the provision of new fireplaces are examined more closely in chapter 7 of this book).

When faced with the constraints of existing conditions and materials, and especially when historic appearance must be preserved, the task of providing efficient, low-cost heating can become more difficult to achieve, and, indeed, sometimes it may appear almost impossible. However, with a certain amount of ingenuity in making use of the conditions available and with a discerning choice of appliance, successful results can be obtained, especially if the characteristics of construction of each historic period are understood and typical defects recognized, and if there is a reasonable knowledge of what the available choice is.

The first of these aspects has been dealt with in the preceding chapters, and it is the second one with which this chapter is concerned. In view of the great variety of appliances available on the market, a detailed account would develop into a subject in its own right, in need of continuous revision, as old products are discontinued and new ones become available. (Information is available from the Solid Fuel Advisory Service area offices and the National Fireplace Council, both of whom update their files regularly.)

Consequently, only the general principles of operation and the range of application are considered here, with some typical examples illustrated in the Product Information Sheets (pp. 145 ff).

All heating appliances consist of a heat source enclosed to varying degrees in a container, which differs in shape depending on the fuel to be used and the efficiency aimed at. With the traditional source of a fire of wood or coal, burning in an open container and radiating heat into the room, there were disadvantages. Such fires burned large quantities of fuel and required considerable air changes in order to function. At the same time a great proportion of the heat produced was lost through the movement of air up the chimney and by absorption into the masonry of the recess.

To overcome these problems and to comply with legislation protecting the atmosphere from pollution, the basic open fire has been steadily improved and developed over the years to enable us to enjoy its benefits to the full without the discomforts associated with it in the past.

In choosing a suitable appliance there are two basic decisions to be made, and while they can be considered almost independently of each other, they must both take into account the conditions of the building they concern.

The decisions are:

1 What type of fuel to use?
2 How is the heat going to be released into the room and throughout the building?

The types of fuel available

While fireplaces have traditionally burnt wood or coal, it may be useful to examine these established fuels in the context of the modern general choice as influenced by the changing availability pattern. An understanding of the characteristics of each type of fuel will not only help in using a fuel judiciously, but will also widen the spectrum of their use, as it is now possible to convert a fireplace by incorporating modern appliances which burn alternative fuels.

To be able to make the correct alterations, so that the adaptation does not affect the existing fabric, it is necessary to be familiar with these fuels and for this purpose they are outlined below in comparison with the traditional ones.

CLASSIFICATION OF FUEL TYPES

There are many ways of classifying fuel, but probably the broadest terms refer to its origins, which enable it to be classified into the following types:

1 Fossil fuels, resulting from geological formation:
Solid fuels (coal and its derivatives)
Gas
Oil

2 Renewable resources:
Solar, tidal, wind and wave power
Organic waste
Wood

3 Electricity, produced mostly from fossil fuels and nuclear energy:
Research is attempting to increase the use of renewable resources, especially as the alternative, nuclear power, is becoming increasingly controversial.

AVAILABILITY OF FUELS

In terms of present and long-term availability, the practical choice is as follows:

NATURAL GAS

Supplies of North Sea Gas, although still large, will probably last only half way through the next century at the present rate of consumption. However, Britain's large coal deposits will permit the development of coal gas when the natural gas supplies have been exhausted.

Advantages
Storage and handling equipment are not required

Disadvantages
A flue for the disposal of combustion products is required
With air it forms an explosive mix

Where a piped supply is available, gas is still cheap, but running costs compare with electricity in remote areas.

OIL

At the present rate of use, even with the help of North Sea deposits, oil is largely an imported commodity from limited reserves and repeatedly associated with supply problems.

Advantages
Can be used in any type of location provided that adequate storage facilities are available
In the past the main attraction was its low cost, but this is no longer the case

Disadvantages
Relatively high installation costs requiring storage tanks, pumps, etc
Supply relies on regular deliveries
Requires flue and special anti-corrosive lining
Can cause condensation problems.

ELECTRICITY

As a direct source electricity is expensive in terms of running costs, but it involves a low capital outlay. It could become competitive again once an alternative power source such as the renewable type of fuels is developed.

Advantages
Clean, no storage or delivery problems, (except of course industrial relations or temporary cuts)
No flues or special construction required

Disadvantages
Expensive, especially if off-peak supplies are not used.

SOLID FUEL — COAL

Britain has abundant reserves of coal, sufficient to last at the present rate of consumption for some three hundred years. Constant improvements in mining technology and appliance construction enable us increasingly to make better use of these supplies.

Advantages
One of the cheapest fuels available
Requires little maintenance
Good ventilation is provided in association with its use
Less likely to cause condensation due to smaller temperature variations made possible by heat storage effect of the surrounding fabric which, when heated gradually, remains warm and radiates heat for some time

Disadvantages
Requires storage facilities and regular deliveries
Appliances mostly have to be stoked manually
Requires flue and chimney
Regular maintenance is needed to cope with products of combustion (ash, soot, etc) in rooms and flues
Most urban areas allow only smokeless fuels to be burned, and this can affect cost and flexibility.

Coal is either bituminous (untreated) or smokeless. Of the *bituminous* type, the best known is housecoal, which, while unsuitable for use in smokeless areas, is cheap, ignites easily and burns with a bright flame. It comes in three progressively cheaper qualities, trebles, large nut doubles and nuts, and is good value for open fires. (Recently developed heaters like the Rayburn Coalglo room heater can now burn it smokelessly.)

There is a very wide range of *smokeless fuels* (natural or manufactured), in various forms to suit most types of appliances. When choosing, account should be taken of the local coal-merchant's advice as well as of the recommendation of the manufacturer of the appliance. Two smokeless fuels especially suitable for open fires are Homefire (a manufactured smokeless version of housecoal) and Coalite, a manufactured carbonized smokeless fuel.

For room heaters and other closed appliances, due to their slow burning qualities, the following smokeless fuels are suitable:

Anthracite and Welsh Dry Steam Coal: naturally smokeless with high heat content, Sunbrite: the most common manufactured smokeless fuel, and Phurnacite: very dense fuel, manufactured from Welsh Dry Steam Coal, smokeless.

SOLID FUEL – WOOD

The area of trees growing in Britain has been steadily increasing and is approaching a total of 5,500,000 acres. In commercial cultivation and production, an estimated 40% of tree growth is wasted by being burnt on site or left to rot. Should use be made of this wood as fuel, it would not only help to preserve coal and oil, but would produce additional income, which could be used to develop improved silvicultural methods and reduce wastage.

Advantages
Relatively cheap
A renewable energy source. This is a characteristic which should be observed by those burning wood for heating. Stripping the land of trees causes moisture loss which in turn leads to soil erosion. The use of wood must therefore be accompanied by methodical replanting, and it is worth noting that the Forestry Commission actively provides technical and professional assistance as well as grants to owners for the maintenance of existing woodlands and the planting of new ones.

Disadvantages
Wood burning is prohibited in smoke-controlled areas. This may be reconsidered in future legislation. (Wood smoke does not contain sulphur oxides as coal smoke does, and it is claimed that wood burning can make a small beneficial ecological contribution in stabilizing the Earth's carbon dioxide concentration.)

Wood is bulky to store (a volume of approximately 700 cubic feet of stacked wood being necessary for the heating of an average three-bedroom house for one year, with further space required for cutting and drying).

There are many 'tricks of the trade' involved in using wood as a fuel, accumulated through past experience or personal preferences, and anybody contemplating wood burning should investigate further. Detailed advice is availabe from WARM (Wood burning Association of Retailers and Manufacturers – see details on p. 143) and the Forestry Commission. There are numerous publications examining the subject in detail, some of which have been listed at the end of this book.

Some useful tips are:
- Hardwood burns better than softwood
- Dry wood burns better than green wood
- It is easier to split green hardwood than dry softwood
- Minimum of six months (preferably twelve months) is required to achieve reasonably dry wood, provided it has been correctly stacked to allow sufficient air circulation between logs
- There is a variety of alternative sources of supply which should not be ignored, for example: off-cuts from wood merchants; limb and tree thinning in woodlands (contact local tree surgeon or tree cutters); sawmill trimmings; diseased elms; wind throws; furniture manufacturers; timber yards and demolition contractors. The Forestry Commission still enters into 'lop and top' agreements in certain areas.

EFFICIENCY

In terms of 'value for money' fuels can be compared by examining the cost of each thermal unit produced. The greater the heating value obtained from the same weight unit of fuel, the more efficiently is that fuel used, and this depends a great deal on the type of appliance used. For example, while in an old-fashioned open fire only 10-14% of the thermal value of, say, wood is used, there are now closed wood-burning appliances on the market whose manufacturers claim a 70% efficiency.

The thermal value in use of a fuel represents the extent to which the potential thermal value of that fuel can be exploited. This depends on the nature of the fuel, the way each particular appliance is supplied and how efficiently the appliance controls air movement and combustion.

A general guide of average figures is given below, but as mentioned before, values vary greatly with the type of appliance.

Fuel	Potential thermal value	Thermal value in use
Wood (air dry)	150 therm/tonne	82.5 therm/tonne
Coal (household)	270 therm/tonne	162 therm/tonne
Anthracite	310 therm/tonne	182 therm/tonne
Oil (domestic)	1.65 therm/gallon	1.07 therm/gallon
Gas	1 therm/therm input	0.7 therm/therm input
Electricity	0.03412 therm/kwh	0.03412 therm/kwh

Note As a rule of thumb, various fuels burn with varying efficiency in relation to their 100% potential, for example

Wood:	55%
Coal:	60%
Oil:	65%
Gas:	70%

When considering a certain type of fuel an idea of the cost involved can be obtained by applying the following general formula:

$$\frac{\text{Cost/Weight unit of fuel}}{\text{Thermal value in use/weight unit}} = \text{Cost/Kwh/therm}$$

For example:

$$\frac{£20/\text{tonne dry wood}}{82.5 \text{ therm/tonne}} = 24.2\text{p/Kwh therm}$$

NB approximately 600 therms are needed annually to heat a three-bedroom house.

Conclusion

In spite of the extensive research campaign brought on by the energy crisis, there is no conclusive evidence to indicate whether a particular type of fuel available today will continue to be available at an economic price in the future. If a way can be found to use alternative renewable resources to generate electricity, this could be the fuel of the future. In the meantime, coal or wood could be the answer if a flue and storage are available, gas if a piped supply is within reach and oil, bottled gas, coal or wood if in a remote location. As far as a general policy is concerned, the best recommendation that can be made at the moment is to avoid, as much as possible, total commitment to a single energy source and consider flexibility essential.

6
Modern appliances

Principles of operation

The first step towards choosing a heating appliance has been made by selecting a preferred type of fuel. In this book, which is concerned with the re-use of existing fireplaces and the introduction of new ones, only the fuels best suited to these purposes will be considered and referred to in association with the appliances discussed. They are solid fuel, wood and gas.

To be able to appreciate what an appliance can offer, its function and basic principles of operation must be understood. The role of a room heating appliance is to burn fuel efficiently and safely and to transmit as much as possible of the heat generated into the room. There are therefore three elements to consider: combustion, judicious construction, maximized transmission of heat.

I   COMBUSTION

To burn efficiently, all fuels require an adequate supply of air, in two forms:

Primary air supply provides the oxygen necessary for the combustion of the fire bed, to which it should be directly aimed.

When the fuel starts to burn two things occur: first, all the moisture is driven out of the fuel and, with the aid of heat, all the natural resins and oils are turned into volatile combustible gases. Secondly, the same heat warms up the column of air above the fire bed (in the flue) which, having so become lighter, attempts to rise carrying away the products of combustion (smoke, soot, etc) in an upward draught movement. The efficiency of this draught depends on the difference in weight between the rising column of warm air and the cold air outside which is displaced as a result of the difference of pressure created.

It is at this point that more air is needed and this usually comes in the form of a secondary air supply.

Secondary air supply is aimed at the flue, passes over the fire bed and has two main functions: first to supply the air necessary for the combustion of the volatile gases and charcoal, which contain about 50% of the fuel's potential heat value, and secondly to enable the column of warm air to rise, promoting an upward draught.

If at this stage the secondary air supply is insufficient (often due to air-tight modern rooms), the warm air will be unable to displace the cold air outside and will be sucked back into the room, filling it with smoke. Similarly, the volatile gases will fail to ignite, and, apart from losing a considerable amount of potential heat as they are driven up the flue, they can also create damage by chemically affecting the inside of the flue as they condense in contact with cold surfaces.

It is therefore important to ensure that both these supplies are adequate and properly balanced in relation to each other, so that efficient combustion may occur. Modern appliances now offer means of draught adjustment for both primary and secondary air supplies, thus facilitating the control of the rate of combustion to suit any requirement. For instance, most room heaters can now be adjusted for over-night slow burning as well as for faster day-time burning. To start with however, heating appliances must be so constructed and installed that maximum combustion efficiency is possible.

2   JUDICIOUS CONSTRUCTION

To function efficiently, heating appliances must be located and equipped judiciously. The fireplace and flue must be constructed in accordance with the time-tested principles examined more closely in chapter 7, which deals with the construction of new fireplaces and flues, outlining the way in which they should be built to be safe structurally, safe in terms of fire resistance and weather proof.

The shape and dimensions of all the components (opening, flue, container) and their connections to each other must be conducive to the upward air movement discussed earlier, minimizing friction with the help of aerodynamic shapes (see fig. 7.1).

Correctly positioned and dimensioned outlets, equipped with draught control devices (usually called dampers) and flexible connection facilities are essential, especially as general conditions differ from case to case. They depend on factors such as the size of the room, the location of the building and flue outlet, and many others. Off-the-shelf appliances are usually designed for average situations, and in special cases (eg very large or small rooms) the availability of adjustment facilities can be vital, especially in the case of an existing fireplace and flue.

3   MAXIMUM HEAT TRANSMISSION

Having ensured efficient combustion, the next objective is to make use of as much of the heat produced as possible. This can be achieved by: avoiding heat loss and maximizing heat absorption.

Heat loss can be avoided by:

● The provision of adequate thermal insulation which can prevent the cooling of the flue. (A cold flue can cause the condensation of the volatile gases mentioned earlier, with the consequent loss of heat potential.)

- An internal location of the fireplace and flue. If possible this is obviously preferable to an external wall position.

- Using an appliance so constructed that it prevents the absorption of heat into the masonry back or recess. This can be achieved by fitting an insulaated fireback which reflects heat into the room, or an insulated casement forming a convection chamber or a back boiler which will make use of heat to warm air or water.

Heat absorption can be maximized by:

- Extending the route of volatile gases as much as possible before they are released outside, and putting them into contact with more radiating metal. This is usually achieved by causing the hot gases and air to circulate longer in areas where they can release more heat, with the aid of insulated convection chambers at the back of the fire (which will also stop the heat from being absorbed into the masonry), baffles (which will create a maze effect stopping the heat from escaping up the chimney) and an air-tight construction (which will prevent leakage); see also Product Information Sheets 1, 2, 3.

- Using appliances constructed of heat-conducting materials.

- Combining direct radiation heat with alternative carriers like air or water. Some convection can be achieved with a simple 'tube grate', constructed of hollow tubes to draw cool air at the bottom and release hot air at the top; see Product Information Sheet 1.

Appliances available

From the point of view of their operation, heating appliances can be classified in three main groups: open, semi-open or completely closed, ie open fires, room heaters (stoves) and independent boilers. The main distinction between these types lies basically in the degree to which the fire bed container is open into the building.

OPEN FIRES

Today open fires can still offer the attraction and warmth of a real fire but without many of the past disadvantages. Modern research has found ways of increasingly improving the basic open fire, and has developed it to a very high degree of efficiency. As a result of the energy crisis, there is now a great choice of appliances available, the construction of which takes into account, as much as possible, costs and availability of fuel as well as the principles on which efficient combustion and heat extraction are based.

Modern designs make fires easier to light and cleaner to burn and maintain. A typical open fire (see fig. 6.1) can be fitted with a deep under-floor ash can (see fig. 6.2), which only needs emptying once or twice a week. In some models it can be removed without disturbing the fire bed, either by rotation of the can to the front or from the outside if the location of the fireplace permits it (see Product Information Sheet 1, fig. 6.2). Alternatively, a deep ash can can be provided at floor level with a raised hearth (see fig. 6.3).

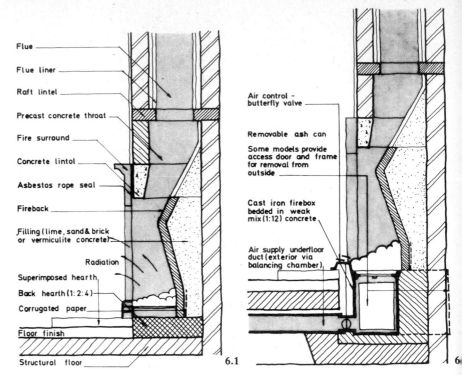

6.1 Traditional open fire construction.

6.2 Open fire with deep under-floor ash can.
There are models available in which the can rotates and can be removed at the front without disturbing the fire bed or, if the building permits it, from outside, through an opening at the back.

Labels for figure 6.1 (left):
Flue
Flue liner
Raft lintel
Precast concrete throat
Fire surround
Concrete lintol
Asbestos rope seal
Fireback
Filling (lime, sand & brick or vermiculite concrete)
Radiation
Superimposed hearth
Back hearth (1:2:4)
Corrugated paper
Floor finish
Structural floor
6.1

Labels for figure 6.2 (right):
Air control – butterfly valve
Removable ash can
Some models provide access door and frame for removal from outside
Cast iron firebox bedded in weak mix (1:12) concrete
Air supply underfloor duct (exterior via balancing chamber)
6

Real fires can now be used much more efficiently than in the past by making use of the heat at the back of the fire which is often lost through absorption in the masonry. Many heating appliances nowadays are equipped with additional fittings (separately or in combination) such as:

Convection chamber An enclosed space at the back of a metal fire bed container, through which air, usually introduced at the sides of the fire, circulates and is released warmer into the room (see fig. 6.4).

Back boiler Here, with the aid of a damper control, hot gases are directed around a metal water container and heat it (see fig. 6.5). The boiler can provide hot water for domestic use or it may heat a small number of radiators provided these can be located near by.

Open fires will burn a wide range of fuels such as bituminous coal, wood, or peat, but under the Clean Air Act these are not suitable for smokeless areas, where manufactured fuels like Homefire, Royal or Coalite are recommended. Detailed advice on the fuel most suitable for a particular appliance can be obtained from the manufacturer, Solid Fuel Advisory Service regional offices and Local Authority environmental health departments.

Not all open fires are suitable for the use of slow burning fuels such as coke or anthracite, and if a slow all-night fire is wanted the appliance chosen must have a suitable grate (see next section) and an adjustable vertical depth of fire bed.

Some appliances are constructed so that a fast burning fuel can be burned during the day and a slow burning fuel during the night.

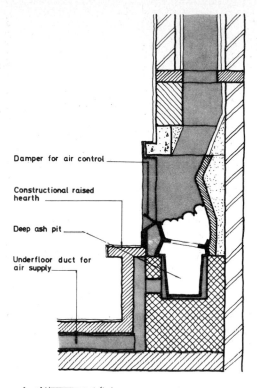

Damper for air control

Constructional raised hearth

Deep ash pit

Underfloor duct for air supply

6.3 Open fire with raised hearth level known as the 'hole in the wall' fireplace.

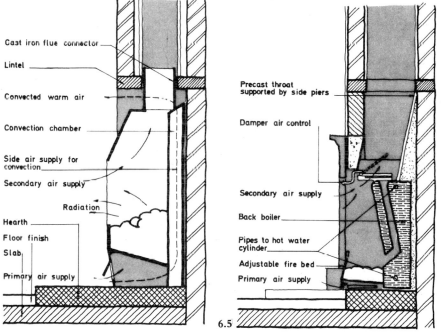

Cast iron flue connector

Lintel

Convected warm air

Convection chamber

Side air supply for convection

Secondary air supply

Radiation

Hearth

Floor finish

Slab

Primary air supply

6.5

Precast throat supported by side piers

Damper air control

Secondary air supply

Back boiler

Pipes to hot water cylinder

Adjustable fire bed

Primary air supply

6.4 Open fire fitted with a convection chamber at the back.

6.5 Open fire fitted with a back boiler.

Others rely on the help of an under-floor air supply, (see fig. 6.2), or a fan to adjust the rate of burning for day or night as required.

ROOM HEATERS (STOVES)

Even in improved form, open fires remain subject to some heat loss through the surrounding structure by the nature of their construction. Room heaters go a step further by enclosing a fire almost completely, using the continental stove principle. Whether closed or with an openable front revealing the fire, the stove's heat is distributed through the radiation of the metal container and by the convection of the air surrounding it. The more enclosed the room heater is, the more efficient it will be. In fact it can be so efficient that in certain cases, especially when completely closed, it must be restricted to a smokeless type of fuel to avoid an almost immediate soot blockage, which would occur when bituminous coal or wood were used.

Recently, however, a new type of room heater has been developed to burn ordinary housecoal smokelessly, thus allowing the use of a cheap bituminous coal in a high-efficiency appliance, even in areas controlled by the Clean Air Acts (see Product Information Sheet 2).

When fitted with a high-output boiler, room heaters can supply very efficient central heating systems (of up to ten radiators), which can be fitted with time switches and thermostatically controlled. If they are to be used to provide the domestic hot water as well, these systems are never completely turned off, which can be uncomfortable in the warm months, but by keeping the fabric of the house warm, they have the added benefit of reducing condensation problems and ensuring a rapid heat-up when this is required.

It is now possible to extend an existing hot water central heating system supplied by an oil- or gas-fired boiler by supplementing it with the hot water from an additional back-boiler attached to an open fire or room heater. This system, known as a 'link-up' system, can allow a great deal of flexibility, not only in costs and fuel availability, but also in heating level adjustments and diversity of use. Not all houses are suitable for this type of system; in some cases, due to the plan layout, the distance between the fireplace and an existing hot water cylinder or central heating link point may be too great, or it may not be possible to provide individual chimneys for every necessary appliance. The advice of a specialist heating engineer should be sought as well as that of a registered heating contractor before attempting installation. The SFAS, CIBS and the Heating and Ventilating Contractors Association should be able to recommend both.

Room heaters are usually freestanding and can be installed in varying conditions ranging from new buildings with specially designed components to old ones with adapted existing fireplaces and flues. Both situations are discussed below.

The room heater principle is also used by wood burning stoves where the advantage of a cheap fuel is somewhat counteracted by the need to follow a fairly rigorous maintenance check list, as outlined below:

1   Only seasoned wood should be burned.
2   The flue must be well insulated and regularly cleaned (see maintenance checklist, p. 126).
3   The fire bed must be properly laid and layered to allow it to start burning efficiently to its full depth. This is not particularly difficult to achieve, provided that the bed is layered of materials which increase in density from the bottom up. For example: screwed up

newspapers at the bottom (these can be put over the previous fire's ash, if the vents are clear), followed by kindling, small wood and finally well seasoned large logs.

NB In an enclosed box, wood will burn from front to rear like a cigar and not from bottom to top as in an open fire, due to the differing direction of the primary air supply.

4   Fire beds must be regularly refuelled, and the correct moment for this must be recognized by observing the progress of the fire. Thus, to begin with there will be long bright flames appearing not to touch the wood, then, as the heat builds up, yellow flames accompanied by grey-white smoke will take over. As the fire continues to burn, the yellow flames will be replaced by smaller white flames from the wood igniting below. Eventually the white flames fade and there will be just a red glow which is the moment when the maximum heat is produced. When the red begins to dim and becomes patched with black, the time for refuelling has come.

INDEPENDENT BOILERS

The domestic boiler is a totally enclosed, highly efficient stove with a back boiler supplying the hot water for heating.

The gap between a room heater and a boiler is becoming smaller and smaller these days as the former becomes more efficient and versatile and the latter less cumbersome to install and operate on a small scale. Boilers can now be fitted easily in a kitchen as a wide range of sizes related to varying heating requirements is available. They burn a variety of fuels suitable for smoke controlled areas and, subject to suitable adjustments, can be fitted into existing flues. There are many devices available which ease maintenance, such as gravity-feed systems which reduce the re-fuelling frequency and deep ash-pans which do not need emptying more than once or twice a week.

In view of their high output, independent boilers are subject to strict statutory controls (see Appendix I) and specialist advice is essential in their selection and installation. Having decided upon the type of fuel and service required, before selecting an appliance, consult the lists of approved appliances closely monitored by the statutory authorities and advisory boards.

Installation of appliances★

To be able to function, open fire appliances will require a hearth, (which can be with or without an enclosing masonry recess), a flue or chimney and a fuel store.

These can be provided as follows:

Custom built as part of a new building or as an independent structure added to an existing building. In both cases, the basic principles of fireplace construction can be combined with the specific conditions

---

★The installation of appliances requires specialist knowledge and should not be attempted without professional advice. For further information on this subject see introduction to chapter 3, p. 60 and Appendix I.

and preferences of a particular situation at the early design stage. (See chapter 7 for new fireplace design.)

Re-use or adaptation of existing fireplaces and chimneys. When old structures are being re-used for modern appliances they should first be examined and then refurbished if necessary as outlined for the traditional open fire (chapter 3), the same principles of operation as originally being maintained in general terms.

In view of the increased efficiency and the additional features of modern appliances, existing structures may need to be adapted to enable them to cope with more demanding functional characteristics.

The aspects to consider from this point of view are as follows:

COMPLIANCE WITH CURRENT LEGISLATION

As in the case of new fireplaces, current legislation is concerned with the construction elements, which must be structurally sound and safe in terms of fire risks; these are under the jurisdiction of Building Control Sections of the Local Authority Planning Departments. Depending on the extent of the alterations required, Planning Permission and Building Regulations Approval may be needed before work begins. (See Appendix I for further details.) If the external appearance of the house will not be affected, there are no structural alterations to the existing fabric and a new structure is not proposed, statutory consents may not be required.

The type of fuel which can be burnt in a certain area is subject to control under the Clean Air Acts, and details of the smokeless zones must be obtained from the Local Authority before proceeding with the installation.

SUITABLE POSITIONING OF THE APPLIANCE

A suitable position will depend on the flexibility of the appliance itself, existing conditions and personal preference.

Room heaters are generally freestanding and can be fitted in an existing recess, using what is known as the 'free inset' method of installation, when a modified form of surround allows the use of additional heat by convection. A superimposed hearth may be required.

Appliances can be almost completely recessed as in fig. 6.6a and sealed directly into the chimney with the aid of a custom-built concrete lintel. This requires the appliance to have a top flue connection. A special metal sheet or other incombustible infill panel can be fitted around the heater and by incorporating adjustable air inlets in the panel the recess space can be utilized as a convection chamber, where air is warmed up before being returned into the room. If this is not possible, the space is usually filled with vermiculite concrete.

Semi-recessed appliances can make use of the existing fire back and be connected directly into the flue, (as in fig. 6.6b) or they can be sealed

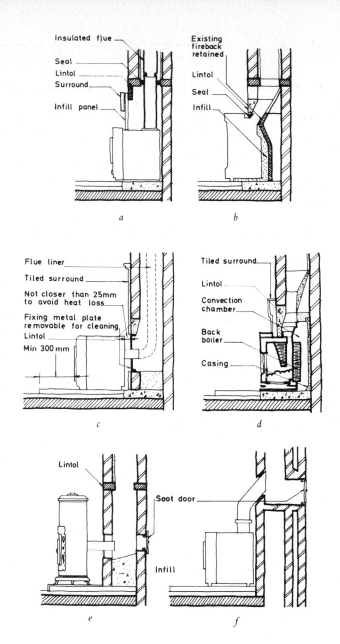

Insulated flue
Seal
Lintol
Surround
Infill panel

Existing fireback retained
Lintol
Seal
Infill

a

b

Flue liner
Tiled surround
Not closer than 25mm to avoid heat loss
Fixing metal plate removable for cleaning
Lintol
Min 300 mm

Tiled surround
Lintol
Convection chamber
Back boiler
Casing

c

d

Lintol

Soot door

Infill

e

f

6.6 Installation of room-heaters.

a Free-standing room-heater with top flue connection, completely recessed in an existing fireplace. The front opening has been sealed with the aid of an infill panel.

b Free-standing room-heater, semi-recessed in an existing fireplace connected directly to the flue shaft.

c Free-standing room-heater with back flue connection installed at the front of an existing fireplace recess.

d Free-standing room-heater with back boiler, semi-recessed in an existing fireplace. The existing fireback has been removed and an insulated casing fitted to form a convection chamber. The front opening is sealed by a purpose-built surround, and the connection to the flue shaft is made with the aid of special link pieces.

e Free-standing room-heater with back flue connection, installed without recess.

f Free-standing room-heater installed without a recess and with a top flue connection.

in with the aid of a purpose built surround and connection pieces, (as in fig. 6.6c).

Appliances can also be installed *without a fireplace recess*, in which case they will require a back flue type connection, (as in fig. 6.6d, 7.2f) or an angle piece added to a top flue, (as in fig. 7.2e).

In all cases care must be taken not only in selecting the appliance best suited to the existing conditions, but also in following closely the manufacturer's installation instructions.

ADEQUATE PROVISIONS FOR SMOKE DISPOSAL

Flues must be aerodynamically shaped for smoke issue (see pp. 119

113

g

g, h A typical installation in an existing chimney.

and 124), airtight and well insulated to avoid loss of heat and condensation of the flue gases. The more efficient appliances are, the better they burn and the more heat they release, which could very quickly wear out an old chimney if it has not been suitably adapted.

Old fireplaces were built to cope with the burning of wood or bituminous coal on open fires. When man-made solid fuels, oil or gas are burned, the chemical reaction of the flue gases at very high temperatures will very quickly corrode old masonry, and, apart from the structural damage, much of the heating efficiency available will be lost through leakage and condensation.

Most flue construction requirements can be met by the provision of flue liners. (Specialist advice must be sought from advisory bodies (see p. 60 and Appendix I) and manufacturers to establish whether a flue liner is needed and what type would be most appropriate for a particular fuel and appliance.) A lining will not only help to protect the fabric of the chimney, but will also make it possible to adjust the size of an existing flue if it is too large. (See chapter 7 for recommended sizes.)

The many types of liners available can be grouped in the following categories:

1   Prefabricated rigid pipes
These can be manufactured from a variety of materials and are usually made in rebated and socketed sections which should be

pointed at the joints with cement mortar. Sockets must be placed uppermost (see fig. 6.7) to prevent rain or condensation ingress. Flue pipes should be supported, if possible, by bricks projecting on the inside of the chimney and must be well insulated either by an air space tightly sealed at both ends, light-weight concrete infill or light-weight insulation wrapping. Some of the types available are:

Asbestos cement pipes
Light quality, suitable for gas
Heavy quality, treated with acid resistant compound, suitable for oil and gas.

Both light and heavy quality, when used in association with a gas burner, are subject to restrictions, and the advice of the Gas Corporation must be sought before attempting installation.

This type of pipe can also be used with solid fuel, but only within 1.8m of the flue outlet of the closed solid fuel appliance (*not* suitable for open fires). They are good for straight flues, where they can be fitted in long lengths, thereby not requiring much opening-up for installation. Joints should be pointed with 1:3 cement/sand mortar with heavy quality pipes and asbestos string caulking with light quality pipes.

Impervious clay pipes
These have a very good resistance to chemical attack, but they are difficult to install as extensive opening-up for jointing is required, which can be expensive.

Refractory concrete pipes
Similar to impervious clay, but with less resistance to chemical attack.

2 Concreted flue blocks
Flue blocks are manufactured from kiln burnt aggregate and high alumina cement. They can be used for solid fuel and oil provided that they are enclosed by a surround of 100mm minimum thickness. They can also be used with gas burners, but in this case, further steps must be taken in protecting the surface to avoid plaster cracks and staining. Joints must be executed very carefully in high alumina cement, so that no excess mortar is allowed on the internal surface.

3 Flexible metal flue liners
These are suitable only for oil and gas fires and *not* for solid fuel appliances, which can make metal liners disintegrate. Easy to install, metal liners can be lowered from the top without opening up the flue, which makes them suitable for use in existing chimneys, especially if they have awkward offsets. (See fig. 6.8 for fixing.)

Flexible metal flue linings are available in two common types: plain steel or aluminium and in a composite of aluminium and lead (used for gas-fired boilers), or aluminium outer layers separated by a building paper infill. Aluminium liners are not suitable in highly corrosive situations.

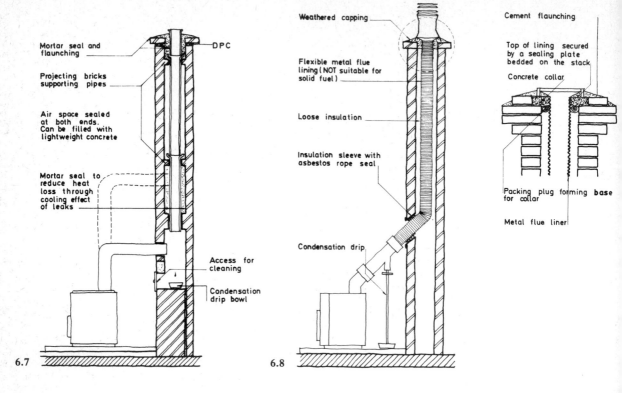

Figure 6.7 labels:
- Mortar seal and flaunching
- DPC
- Projecting bricks supporting pipes
- Air space sealed at both ends. Can be filled with lightweight concrete
- Mortar seal to reduce heat loss through cooling effect of leaks
- Access for cleaning
- Condensation drip bowl

Figure 6.8 labels:
- Weathered capping
- Flexible metal flue lining (NOT suitable for solid fuel)
- Loose insulation
- Insulation sleeve with asbestos rope seal
- Condensation drip

Detail labels:
- Cement flaunching
- Top of lining secured by a sealing plate bedded on the stack
- Concrete collar
- Packing plug forming base for collar
- Metal flue liner

6.7 Flue lining – prefabricated rigid pipes.

6.8 Flue lining – flexible metal liner, and detail.

4   In-situ lightweight concrete liners

Suitable for all types of fuel, these are particularly useful with existing flues. They are a cheap and effective way of reducing the size of the flue, providing an inner surface resistant to chemical attack and at the same time strengthening the structure.

The liner is cast in situ by pumping a lightweight compound (concrete with vermiculite aggregate) around a rubber core which has been inflated to the required flue diameter, (see fig. 6.9), and is removed when the concrete has set. A metal plate seal must be fitted as formwork at the base of the new liner. Where the flue changes direction it may be necessary to open up to ensure that the rubber core is correctly positioned at the centre of the flue allowing an equal thickness of infill to be poured all the way around.

This type of liner can be liable to early attacks of condensation and is not totally impervious to flue gases, but in average domestic conditions it is overall an effective and economical way of adapting existing chimneys.

5   Special provisions for domestic boilers

As mentioned earlier, boilers are very efficient closed appliances operating on the basis of slow combustion. If not adequately insulated, they can cause extensive condensation and chemical attack. It is therefore necessary to ensure that the chimneys of domestic boilers have flues provided with:

- adequate thermal insulation
- well-sealed joints

116

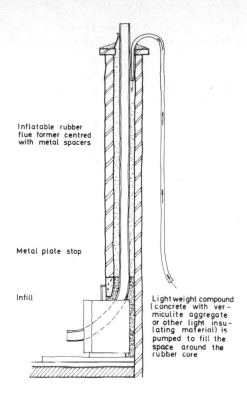

Inflatable rubber
flue former centred
with metal spacers

Metal plate stop

Infill

Lightweight compound
(concrete with ver-
miculite aggregate
or other light insu-
lating material) is
pumped to fill the
space around the
rubber core

6.9 Flue lining – in-situ
light-weight concrete.

- acid-resisting liners
- provisions for the collection and removal of condensation liquid (see container in fig. 6.7)
- provision for air inlets to dilute flue gases; for example, an adjustable grille 1.8m above the flue inlet (for further details, see CP131:101(1954))
- access for regular cleaning.

APPEARANCE

As the performance of heating appliances has altered, so their appearance has also been transformed. There is, of course, a common denominator required by a similar basis of operation involving a hearth, a grate and a flue, but their shape and construction have altered a great deal.

In support of the revival of cheaper alternative fuels such as coal, urged on by the energy crisis, a campaign for a romantic return to the 'Good Old Days' has encouraged a flurry of attempts at adding 'historic' features to modern appliances, sometimes with dubious results.

An aesthetic decision is, of course, a matter of taste, but, when re-using an existing fireplace, certain aspects must be considered in order to avoid incongrous combinations. To a certain extent this is a matter of priorities. If the historic appearance takes precedence one must expect some of the heating standards of the past. If on the other hand, the main objective is to obtain maximum heating efficiency, the historic appearance, more often than not, will suffer.

The jarring aesthetic effect of modern appliances can be less obtrusive if sufficient consideration is given to all aspects involved in installing a new heater in an existing fireplace. For example:

● The existing surround: as much as possible should be retained, and if any of the original features are lost they should be replaced with similar ones.

● The new appliance should have a neutral appearance, easy to blend into the existing background and not competing visually with the original features.

● Installation: the new appliance should be chosen so that it has dimensions as close as possible to the existing opening so that there is no need to alter the original fabric or to cover gaps with in-fill panels.

The advice of a specialist who is independent of the manufacturer or fuel supplier, such as an architect or interior designer specializing in historic restoration, should be sought, as aesthetic decisions are only to a certain extent a matter of personal taste. Much of the process of assessing appearance comes through the experience which is part of the life of professionals such as architects. They have not only come to know and understand the aesthetic characteristics of historic periods, but, being aware of what the market can offer at any particular time, can help to avoid expensive mistakes. Furthermore, as, unlike manufacturers and salesmen, they do not have a vested interest in the sale of a particular appliance, they will be in a position to suggest what is best suited to each situation.

Before beginning the alteration of an existing fireplace, especially in a period house, an expert should be called to advise whether or not one may be dealing with an unusual or rare example. (Suggested experts are: architectural historians, local council's Historic Buildings Officer, museum staff, representative of local conservation group.)

Having decided to proceed with the alterations, and having obtained listed building consent, as much as possible of the old fabric should be retained, care being taken not to destroy any of the original features, such as mouldings, carvings, chimney cranes, hooks, etc, saved during the progress of the works. Care must be taken when removing existing components such as relatively modern grates, as they were often used to provide additional support for the original structure.

Signs of earlier fireplaces, such as old lintels, ovens or built-in seats should be looked for and recorded photographically, as they could give interesting clues not only to the history of the house, but also to the type of chimney construction, which could be useful during the installation of the new appliance.

7
New fireplaces
and their design

To fulfill their function, traditional open fireplaces must provide suitable conditions for the combustion of fuel, the transfer of heat to the room and disposal of smoke and other products of combustion.

Combustion of fuel

The principles of combustion, already defined, indicate that an adequate supply of air is required at two stages: *primary*, bringing oxygen to the fire bed to enable the initial combustion to take place, and *secondary*, directed at the flue and causing the heated air to rise up the flue, carrying away the products of combustion. To achieve this, the fireplace must have a suitable shape, conducive to the necessary upward movement of air. This principle, recognized since the eighteenth century, when Count Rumford applied it to improve the design of fireplaces and grates (see p. 47, fig. 2.15) has remained perfectly valid and can still be used today. It calls for the following points to be observed in the construction of the basic components of the fireplace (the opening, usually a rectangular masonry recess, and the chimney above it):

1 The sides of the fireplace opening should be splayed, (see fig. 7.1). If the front and the back of the opening are equal in width, eddies of smoke can enter the room.

2 The firebed should have sufficient depth, (A in fig. 7.1) to enable the draught to cross the opening without sending smoke into the room on the rebound.

3 The fire back should slope forward. This helps the transition from the large rectangular opening of the fireplace to the smaller one of the flue and, by radiating heat into the room, raises the temperature of the fire, thus aiding combustion.

4 The junction between the fireplace and the flue, known as the 'throat', must be correctly shaped and located. The entrance to the throat must be of a rounded aerodynamic shape to encourage air-draw and is best situated perpendicularly above the fire. Recommended sizes are 100mm wide × 200–250mm long × 150–200mm deep. The throat should be related to the flue and opening size of each particular case: the restriction it provides at the entry into the

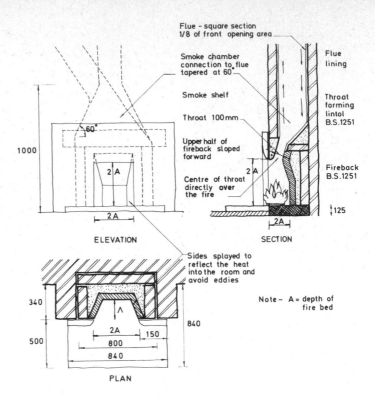

Flue - square section
1/8 of front opening area

Smoke chamber connection to flue tapered at 60°

Smoke shelf

Throat 100 mm

Upper half of fireback sloped forward

Centre of throat directly over the fire

Flue lining

Throat forming lintol B.S.1251

Fireback B.S.1251

125

2A

ELEVATION

SECTION

Sides splayed to reflect the heat into the room and avoid eddies

Note – A = depth of fire bed

340

500

840

2A   150
800
840

PLAN

7.1 Principles of fireplace design for traditional open fires. Dimensions refer to statutory requirements and standard components.

flue will increase the velocity of the air movement.

As discussed in the previous chapter, the control of the air supply to traditional open fireplaces is limited, and use should be made of the various means of reducing heat waste. These can range from the installation of a hood to modern appliances with back boilers, convection chambers and damper controls.

Transfer of heat

To be able to transfer the heat produced by combustion, a fireplace must be constructed of suitable materials, capable of storing and radiating this heat. At the same time, its construction must be:

- structurally sound
- fire resistant
- thermally insulated
- weatherproof.

STRUCTURAL SOUNDNESS AND RESISTANCE TO FIRE

New fireplaces must comply with the standards set by statutory controls, a guide to which is given in Appendix I. As a general guide, the structural components should have the following characteristics:

The hearth must be sound, non-combustible and thick enough to form a fireproof base for the fire. Also, it should extend sufficiently at the front and sides to prevent the spread of fire from the bed. A hearth usually consists of three components:

- the constructional hearth (the incombustible structural base)

think that we are called upon in justice to give a notice of the other, more especially as it is one of very superior merit.

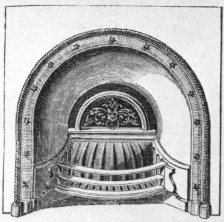

Fig. 1.

The Patent Vesta Register Grate, of which a front view is shown in the annexed engraving (Fig. 1), is designed for the twofold purpose of preventing the undue rush of air into the chimney, and also of reflecting the heat radiated from the fuel into the room, in such directions as to be most advantageous; the first desirable result is accomplished by the register having a central door, which is intended to be kept shut when the fire has burnt up, thus checking the rush of air to the chimney, the outer door, which forms a kind of ring around the inner, being left open sufficiently to carry off the products of combustion without allowing any unnecessary escape of heated air up the chimney. The improvement in the radiating power of the stove is effected by the adoption of a concave radiating arch above the fire, consequently the heat which is radiated from the upper surface of the fire is reflected parallel with the floor, as shown in the vertical section (Fig. 2), instead of being directed towards the ceiling, as is the case with many grates having reflecting surfaces around them. The rays of heat falling on the cheeks or splay sides of the grate, are reflected in a divergent direction into the room, as shown in the horizontal section (Fig. 3), thus the lower part of the apartment is thoroughly and efficiently warmed. From this description it may be seen that the Vesta Stove is one of considerable merit, and we should think likely to meet with very general adoption amongst architects and builders of houses where a better class of grate is in request.

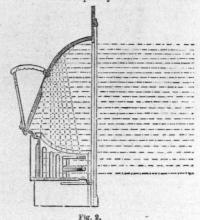

Fig. 2.

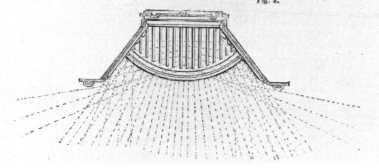

7.2 **Patent Vesta Register Grate** as illustrated in 'The Ironmonger' of 1861 illustrating the incorporation of convection-inducive shapes in the fireplace design.

● the superimposed hearth (also incombustible, usually required as a feature or to reduce the height of the opening)
● the back hearth (the section corresponding to the superimposed hearth contained in the recess).

The recess and surround (not necessary for free-standing appliances), consisting of jambs and back, should be incombustible and thick enough to prevent the heating of their outer surfaces. The recess must also give sound structural support to the chimney breast and the flue.

121

The throat was traditionally formed by a lintel at the front of the fireplace opening, while a corbelled gather made the transition from the recess to the flue section. Nowadays, it is possible to use standard precast throat units with raft or flat lintels above (with a 200mm diameter flue hole) to support the wall and carry the flue. Alternatively a precast throat unit can combine the two functions (see fig. 7.3 for both cases).

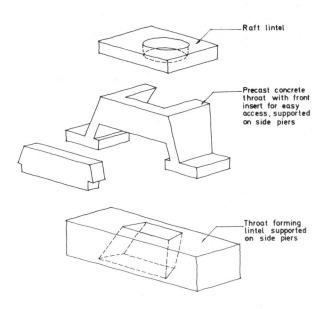

Raft lintel

Precast concrete throat with front insert for easy access, supported on side piers

Throat forming lintel supported on side piers

7.3 Prefabricated throat and lintel units.

 There are Codes of Practice and British Standards giving detailed information for the construction of recess components, the principal ones being CP 403 (1974) and BS 1251:1970.

The flue A chimney rising through the building must be built with sufficient wall thickness (minimum 102.5mm solid brickwork, 200mm if a party wall or 2 × 100mm if a cavity wall) and foundations to be stable and to resist wind pressure above the roof level. Acceptable dimensions and standards of construction are set by statutory requirements which also lay down limitations for the stack height.
 Flues should have no bends if possible, but if changes of direction are made necessary by the shape of the chimney, they should not be abrupt. Internal surfaces should be kept smooth to reduce friction, which will otherwise hinder the upward movement of air.

THERMAL INSULATION

Thermal insulation should be provided around the flue in order to prevent heat loss, cooling-down of the flue and its consequent draught loss and condensation (in contact with cold surfaces, hot flue gases will condense and cause damage to the fabric of the flue). Simply sealing the air space between the wall of the chimney and the lining would not be sufficient; it is preferable to fill this space with insulating materials such as lightweight concrete, mineral wool or noncombustible lightweight insulation filling. See also pp. 114–118 for installation details for different types of liner.

WEATHER PROOFING

Wind and rain must be prevented from entering the flue as they adversely affect its operation and in time erode the fabric, making it structurally unsound.

Wind penetration can be prevented by:

● Judicious location of the flue, away from zones of wind pressure which can cause down-draught, such as on the side of a tall neighbouring tree or building (see fig. 4.18, 4.19).

● Situating outlets (chimney stacks) higher (min. 1.0m) than the roof ridge level and on the leeward side of the prevailing wind. If the pitch of the roof is greater than 30°, the outlet should be positioned as close as possible to the ridge.

● Fitting chimney cowls when unsuitable positions cannot be avoided.

Damp penetration can be prevented by:

● The correct construction of the top of the flue. The traditional method of terminating a flue consists of the installation of a cylindrical fireclay pot (slightly tapered towards the top to increase the velocity of the issuing smoke), which is bedded in one or two courses of brickwork, and covered with a capping of mortar, known as 'flaunching', sloped to throw off water (see fig. 3.4). The top courses of brickwork must be laid on a damp proof course (DPC), which, along with the capping, will help to prevent the saturation of the rest of the brickwork. The flaunching and the top twelve courses should be executed with a strong cement (or cement-lime) mortar mix of 1:1:6, but due to their exposed position, stacks are subject to decay in time and should be regularly maintained. A projecting capping will not only keep the rain water clear of the fabric, but will also help to create a low-pressure zone which will encourage up-draught.

Good alternative flue terminations can be weathered stone or precast caps, which will be easier to install and maintain, or slab caps (see fig. 3.14), which can prevent the entry of rain and some of the directional wind effects.

● Adequate protection at the point where a stack passes through a roof.

This can be achieved by providing the following:

1   lead or copper DPC tray and apron flashing
2   flexible or semi-rigid chimney-back gutter
3   stepped DPCs along the sides with stepped apron flashings which will all ensure that no dampness will penetrate below roof level (see fig. 7.4; also 3.15, 3.16)

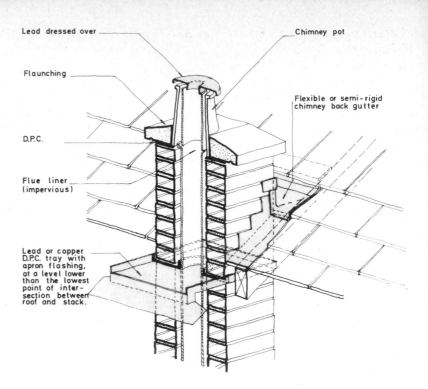

Lead dressed over

Chimney pot

Flaunching

Flexible or semi-rigid
chimney back gutter

D.P.C.

Flue liner
(impervious)

Lead or copper
D.P.C. tray with
apron flashing,
at a level lower
than the lowest
point of inter-
section between
roof and stack.

**7.4 Chimney construction for
the prevention of damp
penetration.**

Disposal of smoke

To dispose of smoke effectively and promote the upward draught
necessary for efficient fuel combustion, flues must be: suitably
located, correctly sized, shaped and constructed, airtight and properly insulated.

Location   .
The location of the flue must be considered so that there is as little
heat loss as possible, preferably on an internal wall
Bends and offsets should be eliminated as far as possible as they
hinder air-flow
The top of the flue must not be in a down-draught position.

Size, shape and construction
The size, shape and construction of the flue must facilitate airflow.
Chimneys must be structurally stable and must comply with statutory requirements concerning the relationship between their height
and plan section. As a general rule, to function effectively a chimney
should not be shorter than 4m measured vertically from the outlet of
the appliance or fireplace to the outlet of the flue.

An adequate height will ensure an adequate difference in weight
between the warm flue gases and the cold air outside – discussed in
association with the principles of combustion, (see p. 105). Requirements vary throughout the British Isles, depending on the position in
the building. Similarly the height of the outlet above the roof should
be limited to a minimum of 600mm to ensure good clearance and to a
maximum of 4.5 times its horizontal dimension for stability.

The plan section of the flue must be related to the size of the fireplace opening. The correct proportion between the size of the fireplace and the size of the flue is the most essential feature of an efficient open fire.

There are no hard and fast rules: the size of the fireplace opening depends on the size of the fire bed required, and this in turn depends on the size of the room it is expected to heat. Dimensions recommended by the British Standards refer to average sized habitable rooms, and aim to suit standardized components such as firebacks, flue blocks, etc. Thus, for a standard fire 406 to 457mm wide and 565mm high the opening should be: 328–578mm deep × 585–600mm high. For this reason, in special situations special solutions will be required probably at higher cost, as custom built components may be required.

It will be useless to provide an opening of the recommended proportions if the flue is too large, as the column of air within it will be too heavy to be raised by the heat from the firebed, which is limited by the set opening. Similarly, if the flue is too small, it will fail to promote enough draught to keep the fire going and will become blocked up with the products of the combustion below.

The following figures can be used as starting points: the Solid Fuel Advisory Service recommends that the cross-sectional area of a flue should be ⅛th of the frontal area of a fireplace opening, where the chimney is more than 5m high, and ⅙th if it is under 5m high.

The Building Regulations specify a minimum diameter dimension of 175mm, but this varies with the type of appliance and fuel, (185mm square or 200mm diameter for smokeless fuel).

The correct construction of a flue should also make provisions for restrictive entry and outlet points (which will help to increase the velocity) and a smooth inner surface which will reduce friction. Bends and offsets must be avoided and, if this is not possible, they must be kept to a minimum, with angles no sharper than 60° to the horizontal, and as near to the top as possible.

Air tightness
A flue must be air-tight to be able to promote an adequate draught. Cold air allowed to enter through defective joints or withes (flue dividers) can cause condensation, chemical attack and too much dilution of the hot flue gases.

Insulation
As already explained, good insulation prevents heat loss and condensation. This can be achieved by constructing the chimney with an adequate wall thickness, locating it internally and by installing insulated liners.

Maintenance

All fireplaces need regular maintenance. A routine annual check observing especially those points which are more likely to be affected, and some simple general attendance work is all that is required to maintain problem-free use and to avoid costly reinstatements or repairs.

Checklist

The following points should be checked (refer to the relevant sections of the book for details):

1   Do not vary or change the type of fuel in use without seeking specialist advice from the appliance's manufacturer and/or the local building control officer.

2   Examine the hearth and recess to ensure that they are free of cracks or any other damage that may create a fire risk or encourage heat loss.

3   Examine the chimney, both inside (using a torch) and externally, looking for evidence of chemical staining or condensation. If there is some staining but it is not severe, it may be possible to seal the affected area by applying adhesive-backed foil, foil-backed plasterboard or similar material (see p. 75 for further details).

If the plaster or brickwork has been contaminated, it is best that the decayed sections are cut out and replaced with new materials (after dealing with the cause).

4   Examine the condition of the leadwork at the junction between the stack and the roof. Feel the adjacent timbers from inside the roof to see if any damp is finding its way below the roof covering.

5   Examine the condition of the stack's brickwork and re-point if necessary.

6   Examine the condition of the capping and repair if necessary.

7   Examine the condition of the inside of the flue. Look for blockages and cracks around the liner joints.

8   Have the flue swept once a year or more often if using a modern appliance burning wood or smokeless fuel.

Sweeping

Regular sweeping will ensure that there is no build up of soot in the flue which, apart from causing physical blockage, can, by combining with the tar from burning fuel, create a deposit known as 'creosote'. This, apart from its unpleasant smell, if allowed to build up, can cause damage to the inner lining by chemically attacking it, and can, at high temperatures, ignite and start a chimney fire. It can significantly reduce the diameter of the small flues usually associated with slow burning appliances.

Sweeping is best done by professional sweeps. They use a variety of techniques from the traditional rod and brush, evolved from cane and bristle to polypropylene rods and nylon brushes, to the more modern and cleaner vacuum sweeping which is very effective with small soot deposits.

For blockages or neglected build-ups, the rod and brush method is, however, still the best (see fig. 7.5). Some of the traditional ways, such as pulling a small spruce tree or bunch of holly down through the chimney, can also be useful, especially when there is a need to break the vitrified crust of old creosote deposit which is too hard for

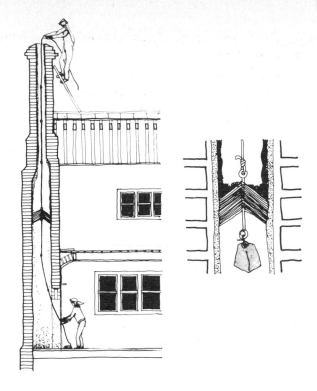

7.5 Rod and brush sweeping.
A weighted brush can damage
the fabric of the chimney.

the brush. This method is also useful when the flue is larger than usual. However, avoid ad-hoc arrangements such as weighted brushes or chains, which can cause damage to the fireplace and the chimney (see p. 68).

A more recent development is the use of chemical cleaners which can be used both as a preventive and as a removing agent. They come in powder or liquid form, can be used with all types of fuel, and when sprinkled onto a hot fire will combine with the carbon in the soot and cause it to peel off. There are several types available, usually imported from countries experienced in wood burning such as Canada or the Scandinavian countries (see Product Sheet 7 for examples).

The build-up of creosote can be reduced by a good design and steps to avoid some of the factors that lead to it. These are chiefly

- *Smoke density*, which can be reduced by diluting with additional air supplies, but care must be taken not to cause:

- *Too low a stack temperature* which causes the flue gases to condense into tar

- *Long passage of the smoke* This is caused by a slack draught and by over-large flues. (The more time the smoke is allowed to circulate through the flue, the more soot will be deposited in it.)

Appendix I
Statutory controls

1 Planning control

PLANNING PERMISSION

Under the Town and Country Planning Act 1971, planning permission is required for carrying out any work which constitutes a development as defined in this Act.

In the case of work for maintenance improvement or alteration of a building, if the work involved entails a *material* change of use or if it would *materially* affect the external appearance of a building, it will constitute a development and therefore will require that planning permission is obtained before the work is carried out.

The construction of a new fireplace will obviously have some effect on the external appearance of a building, but whether it will affect it *materially* would depend on the circumstances of each individual case.

In practice, any improvement to a dwelling house (the insertion of a fireplace, for example) constitutes a development, but in some cases permission can be deemed to have been granted.

Interpretation of the Act tends to vary from one Local Authority to another, so it is best to consult the Local Planning Officer for confirmation as to whether planning permission is required or not.

If permission is necessary, a written application must be made to the Planning Authority by completing the specially prepared forms and payment of the appropriate fee.

LISTED BUILDING CONSENT

Under the Town and Country Planning Act 1971 and the Town and Country Amenities Act 1974, a Listed Building Consent (*as well as* planning permission) must be obtained from the Local Planning Authority when:

(a)   It is proposed to build a new building or demolish the whole or parts of an existing one in a Conservation Area.
(b)   It is proposed to carry out improvement, correction, alteration or demolition work to a building listed, under s.52 of the 1971 Act, as of special historic or architectural interest or to a building which has had a Building Preservation Notice served on it under s.58 of the same Act.

This legislation is designed to preserve and conserve special buildings by discouraging the owners from altering or damaging them. So, it is an offence to demolish, alter or extend a listed building in any 'manner which would affect its character as a building of special architectural or historic interest' internally or externally without first obtaining written consent from the Local Authority. (*NB* A Local Authority can, upon giving the owner seven days' notice, undertake such works as are urgently necessary for the preservation of an *unoccupied* listed building and recover the costs from the owner.)

Owners of historic fireplaces (listed as part of a complete interior or as a specific item) must observe these provisions when considering an alteration or improvement and seek specialist advice before undertaking any modifications.

2 Building control

Under the Public Health Acts of 1936 and 1961 (amended by the Health and Safety at Work Act 1974) building work, structural alterations or extensions of existing buildings can be carried out only if they comply with the Building Regulations 1976 (which have replaced the former Building Byelaws in England and Wales) or the London Building Acts and Byelaws in the Greater London area and the Building Standards (Scotland) (Consolidation) Regulations 1971 to 1979 in Scotland.

The Regulations are designed to safeguard the health, safety, welfare and comfort of persons using a particular building, and do so by setting mandatory requirements for the design and construction of that building.

As for planning permission, application must be made in writing and the appropriate fee paid. In relation to fireplaces, building regulations aim to ensure that the components (chimney, flue, hearth, etc) are so constructed that heat can be provided without endangering the health and safety of the users. Thus they should:

- be incombustible
- prevent the spread of fire
- prevent poisonous gases from entering the house and from being released into the atmosphere.

Among other sections, indirectly related to the position of fireplaces, the following parts of the Building Regulations and Byelaws should be especially observed:

Building Regulations
Part E (Safety in Fire)
Part F (Thermal Insulation)
Part A10 and Schedule 3, rules D and F (give details of the situations in which special consents will be required before any installation work is commenced)

GLC Byelaws
Part XI (Fire Resistance). (It should be noted that in London many of

the special consents that may be required are subject to the District Surveyor's decision.)

Scottish Regulations
Part F (Other Fuels)
Part C (Structural Stability)
Part D (Height of Chimneys)
Part E (Means of Escape in the Case of Fire)
Part J (Thermal Insulation)

To give an idea of the way in which these regulations are structured, a summary of some of the parts relevant to the use of solid fuel fires in the Building Regulations and the GLC Byelaws is given below.

It must be noted that the rules listed are in abbreviated form, intended for guidance only and do not reproduce the actual documents. These are also subject to the interpretation of the local authorities and current legislation.

Fig. 1 gives a diagrammatic illustration of the components affected by statutory controls.

England & Wales	London	Scotland
GENERAL		
L1, L2, L10	12.14, 12.15	F1, F2, F6, F7, F9, F20.
OUTLETS		
L3	12.06	F5, P2
CHIMNEYS & FLUES		
L6	12.01	F3
L9	12.06	F4
L11	12.13	F8
L12		F10
L22		F12
		F 20a
RECESSES & APPLIANCES		
L3	12.07	F13, F14
M1, M7		F18, F19
HEARTHS		
L4	12.02, 12.09	F15
L5	12.10, 12.12	F17

1 Diagrammatic representation of fireplace components subject to statutory controls.

BUILDING REGULATIONS, PARTS L AND M

Part L: Chimneys, fluepipes, hearths and fireplace recesses – constructional requirements:

L1: Defines Class I and high output appliances
Class I – domestic output under 45Kw
(solid fuel and oil)
High output – over 45Kw (gas).

L2: Gives general structural requirements for construction
Must be non-combustible (bricks, concrete blocks, insitu concrete).
Must have adequate thickness and be so placed or protected as to prevent ignition (125mm).
Must not allow any products of combustion to escape internally into the building, be a nuisance to neighbours, or be a health hazard.
Must be provided with suitable access for cleaning.

L3: Fireplace recesses for Class I appliances
Adequate wall thickness related to the appliance position (internal wall, external etc) is required, minimum dimensions are given for each case.[1]

L4: Hearth construction for Class I appliances
Minimum thickness: 125mm
If it is adjoining a combustible floor the appliance must be separated from it by a minimum 150mm wide incombustible section. Also must not be lower than floor level. If enclosed by a recess, the hearth must extend within it and project sufficiently (minimum dimensions given as 500mm in front and 150mm at the sides).
The use of combustible materials is to be restricted in accordance with given limits.
Acceptable ash pit construction is described.

L5: Walls and partitions adjoining Class I appliances
If a free-standing appliance is not in a recess, but on a constructional hearth, the thickness of the wall behind should be a minimum 200mm if solid, 100mm if a cavity wall.

L6: Chimneys and flue linings, Class I appliances
Types and suitable methods of installation are described.
Acceptable dimensions of wall relative to position and section are given.
Suitable construction details for the connection to the appliance are described.

L7/8/9: Flue pipes, usually connecting appliance to chimney, Class I appliances
Describes position and relationship with other building components (floor, roof, walls etc).
Describes 'deemed-to-satisfy' materials and the construction of flue pipes.

L10: Proximity of combustible materials, Class I appliances
No combustible material can be closer to the inner surface of the recess, flue opening or at pipe penetration through wall or floor slab than 200mm (150mm if wooden plug).
Where a non-combustible surround is less than 200mm, only skirting, dado or mantel shelf are allowed, but not closer than 38mm.
No metal fastening in contact with combustible material is allowed to be closer than 50mm to the flue or inner surface of the flue.

---

1 A recent decision of the Secretary of State has established that regulation L3 does not apply to 'through' fireplaces: these were considered to constitute an opening rather than a recess or a recess with an opening at the back (*Building*, 12 August, 1983, p. 49).

L11: Openings into flues, Class I appliances
Openings into flues are permitted only for cleaning, an air inlet or, if internal, at the appliance location, explosion door or draught stabilizer.

L12: Flues to more than one room, Class I appliances
Flues communicating with more than one room are not permitted.

L13: Outlets of flues (chimney stacks)
Their position relative to the roof should be at least 1m above the highest point of contact or 600mm above the ridge if located within 600mm of it. This is intended to control downdraughts or turbulence on discharge from chimney.
Minimum distances relative to windows and other ventilation openings are given.

L22: Insulated metal chimneys, Class I or II appliances
General requirements are given for the construction of metal chimneys.
Joints are not allowed within the thickness of a floor or wall.
If bends are required, they should be not less than 60° angle except where they are connecting into an appliance, where it can be less.
Proximity to combustible materials should be in accordance with BS 4545.
Location restricted to the same building as the appliance.
If in cupboards or stores, chimneys must be encased in accordance with described conditions.

Part M: Heat producing appliances and incinerators
Positioning and installation of appliances and the fuel used are discussed.

M1:   Sets out definitions and areas of application.

M2:   Deals with the prevention of smoke emission (Clean Air Act Provisions).
New buildings (erected under present control) are not allowed to contain appliances which do not burn smokeless fuel (gas, hard coke or anthracite). Therefore, *all solid fuel appliances must be capable of* burning authorized smokeless fuel, regardless of smoke control orders. Open fires are required to burn smokeless fuel only in areas controlled by a smoke control order.

M3:   Covers high rating appliances, (non-domestic) with outputs higher than 45Kw.

M4:   Class I appliances (output less than 45Kw): sets out conditions for their installation. They must
• have adequate air supply for combustion (usually natural air leakage through doors, windows etc is sufficient. CIBS Practice Notes give guidance). See also M7 for deemed-to-satisfy examples (not mandatory)
• be placed on new hearth as before, or if existing, built before present control, new hearth under or superimposed as described
• conform to positioning dimensions given for free-standing

appliances on constructional or superimposed hearth, in a recess, relative to a wall

• conform to conditions for connecting appliances to the chimney or flue

• (with open fires) have securely anchored fire-guard either in the appliance itself or in the adjoining structure.

GLC BUILDING BYELAWS, PART XII

(Flues, chimneys, hearths, ducts and chimney shafts)

XII-1 A separate flue is required for each fire (unless in the same room). Special cases allowed subject to District Surveyor's approval.

XII-2 Proximity to wood and other combustible materials
These are not allowed within 225mm of any flue or back of recess, within 150mm of the sides and 300mm above fireplace opening unless wood plugs, (150mm). They are allowed on the underside of the hearth if there is a minimum 50mm airspace.

XII-3 Flue pipes
Materials and construction details are described. Limits are set for the use of asbestos cement pipes. The position of termination outlet to be in accordance with the requirements set and internal and external conditions are covered.

XII-4 Ducts from cooking and trade appliances
Construction requirements are given – must be read in conjunction with XI.05 and XI.06.

XII-5 Chimney construction
The use of most patent throat units or terminals is permitted.
Cross section should not be less than 150mm in any direction.
Construction requirements, minimum thickness of wall etc. are given.
A lining is required if the output is over 30Kws. Special cases are subject to District Surveyor's approval.
Permits the rendering or plastering of lining. If the chimney has bends of less than 45°, the upper part should be 200mm thick and an adequate cleaning opening must be provided at that point.

XII-6 Chimneys above roofs
Acceptable positions relative to roofs are described. Permitted height relative to the plan section is defined.
Requirements for materials of construction at the top are given.

XII-7 Fireplace openings
Gives minimum construction dimensions for the thickness of party walls at the back of opening and jambs and above.

XII-8 Surrounds
Apart from splayed lintels, all surrounds must be fixed on a minimum 100mm solid, non-combustible backing inside.

XII-9 Hearths in and in front of fireplace openings
Gives construction requirements for hearth (non-combustible, mini-

mum 125mm thick, to extend a minimum 150mm at sides and 500mm at front) and ashpit.

XII-10 Curbs to hearths

These are required where the hearth extends less than 400mm at the front.

Construction details are given (minimum 38mm high, not closer to fire than 300mm).

If there is a superimposed hearth, curbs can be incorporated in it.

XII-11 Rooms or enclosed spaces containing heating appliances

Requires that enclosures, floors or roofs around appliances are of the specified rating or size to be non-combustible or lined with fire-resistant material. Doors must be Class A or protected by Class A materials.

This byelaw does not apply to gas or electricity and must be read in conjunction with Part XIII (oil burning appliances).

XII-12 Hearths under stoves (does not apply to gas or electricity)

Construction details and dimensions are listed.

XII-13 Chimney shafts

Construction requirements are listed for different building materials used externally and internally – brickwork, reinforced concrete etc, leaving specific arrangements subject to District Surveyor's approval.

XII-14 Smoke prevention

Does not apply to buildings begun before 1960. It is in fact an extension of the Clean Air Acts and only appliances using smokeless fuel are permitted.

XII-15 Fire resistance of materials

Defines fire-resistant materials, with reference to Schedules II and III of the London Byelaws. (BS 476, Part 1: 1953 referred to has been superseded by BS 476, Part 7: 1971 and Part 8: 1972.) The District Surveyor can approve other materials at his discretion.

OTHER INFORMATION

In association with the statutory requirements, there are a series of British Standards and Codes of Practice which should be consulted, and are listed on p. 153.

Solid Fuel Advisory Service Publications: The Solid Fuel Heating Compendium

The Property Services Agency (Department of the Environment) and the Building Research Establishment also publish advisory leaflets but, at the time of writing, most were said to be undergoing revision.

3 Other statutory controls

There are many other Acts which may prove relevant in the event of the building of a new fireplace or the adapting of an existing one. Those more commonly encountered are outlined overleaf:

THE CLEAN AIR ACT 1956 AND 1968

This act is designed to make provisions for abating the pollution of air. Among other things, it controls:

- The height of chimneys (section 10) in order to prevent them becoming a nuisance or health hazard.
- The creation of smoke control areas (section 11) restricting the type of fuel and appliances which can be used in a certain area.
- The adaptation of fireplaces (section 12) usually to enable smoke-less fuel to be used.

THE HIGHWAYS ACT 1980

This act, consolidating earlier legislation, controls among other things the frontage line beyond which a building may not project without the Local Authority's consent, as the space may be required for prospective road widening.

This may affect a new chimney breast added to an existing building on the highway side. When in doubt, Local Authority's Highways department should be consulted for advice.

THE FIRE PRECAUTIONS ACT 1971

This Act is concerned with ensuring that adequate precautions are taken in case of a fire and that suitable means of escape in case of a fire are provided in certain types of buildings. (It should be noted that the provisions of this Act are separate from those laid down in Part E of the Building Regulations which deals with safety in fire.) Among others, the following categories of buildings are covered:

- Certain residential establishments (hotels, boarding houses, hospitals).
- Certain private dwellings (usually over two storeys high).
- Licensed premises (restaurants, pubs, clubs, etc).

In practice this involves obtaining a fire certificate from the Fire Authority (County Council).

The installation of open fires (often such an attractive feature in a hotel, pub or restaurant) is a common example of the type of work which could be affected by this Act under the provisions of which it can be held that it creates a fire risk area requiring adequate construction and effective separation from escape routes. It will therefore be helpful to discuss such proposals with the local fire officer before the work is put in hand.

4 Grants

Owners of an existing fireplace or those intending to install a new one may be in a position to obtain financial assistance in the form of a grant or a loan from the Local Authority (the local District or Borough Council) or sometimes, depending on circumstances, from private bodies.

This financial assistance can be mandatory or discretionary and is available by virtue of statutory allowances designed to encourage particular kinds of improvements and conversions.

For the purposes of this book, grants can be grouped into three categories basically following the provisions of the following major Acts:

(a)   The Housing Act 1974, which aims to improve housing conditions.

(b)   The Historic Buildings and Ancient Monuments Act 1953 and The Local Authorities (Historic Buildings) Act 1962 which aim to preserve buildings of special architectural or historic interest.

(c)   The Clean Air Act 1956 (and 1968 amendment) which aims to make provisions for the abating of air pollution.

Grants can be applied for by the owner or occupier of a house. Applications should be in writing (making use when appropriate of the Local Authority's specially prepared forms) *before* the work involved is commenced.
   An outline of the grants available is given below, but in view of their mostly discretionary nature, depending on the circumstances of every particular case, the Local Authority must be consulted for details.

GRANTS AVAILABLE UNDER THE HOUSING ACT 1974

1   Improvement grants for the provision of higher housing standards (discretionary)
   Circular 21/80, Appendix A, para 5 sets a ten-points standards requirement, among which the following could be applicable in the case of the installation of some of the appliances discussed in this book, provided there were no other means of providing the same at the time the application for grant is made.
   vii – satisfactory facilities for preparing and cooking food.
   viii – adequate facilities for heating.

2 Intermediate grants (mandatory) for the provision of standard amenities (minimum standards, to which everyone is entitled) as set by SI 1980, No 1736 amending Schedule 6 of the 1974 Act, to include among others: hot and cold water supply to bath, shower, sink or basin.
   This could be provided with the aid of some of the appliances discussed in the book.

3 Repair grants (discretionary) – for the repair, renovation or replacement of dwellings, usually of a substantial, structural nature and especially in a Housing Action or General Improvement area.

GRANTS AVAILABLE UNDER THE HISTORIC BUILDINGS ACTS 1953 AND 1962

These grants are discretionary, but the owner can apply to several Local Authorities other than that of his district, provided they are in the 'vicinity' (see 1962 Act for details). Grants or loans are available only for repairs and maintenance. There are also certain private bodies which can make funds available for the repair or restoration of historic buildings, but this will not be on a statutory basis so there is no legally enforceable claim to them. Such bodies are: the National Trust, the Historic Buildings Council, Society for the Protection of Ancient Buildings.

The availability of grants in this category could prove of interest to owners of historic fireplaces with, for example, highly decorated chimney stacks in need of structural consolidation or a unique carved surround threatened by fungal or insect infestation, etc.

It should be noted that this legislation concerns only buildings of special architectural or historic interest which are normally listed in accordance with the provisions of the 1971 Town and Country Planning Act. If in doubt advice should be sought from the Local Conservation offices.

GRANTS AVAILABLE UNDER THE CLEAN AIR ACT 1956 AND 1968 AMENDMENT

It is sometimes possible to obtain from the Local Authority a grant (discretionary) towards the cost of making such adaptations to fireplaces as necessary to comply with the requirements of the Clean Air Act 1956, s.512(1), which in effect call for the burning of smokeless fuel in certain areas.

The owner or occupier of a dwelling can claim a grant provided:

(a)   The house was built or produced by conversion of other premises before 16th August 1964.
(b)   The claim is made under the following conditions:

1   The Local Authority has made a smoke control area order (it applies before and after it has come into force).
2   The Local Authority has served a notice requiring the adaptations to be undertaken.

The grant (fixed by s. 12 to a minimum of seven tenths of the expenditure incurred) is allowed only for *necessary* work (not for additional or luxury provisions), which must be carried out to the Local Authority's satisfaction.

The type of work which would qualify can include the following:

1   Adapting or converting a fireplace.
2   Replacing a fireplace with another or with some other means of cooking or heating.
3   Altering a flue or chimney serving a fireplace.
4   Providing ignition (gas, electric or other).
5   Carrying out operations incidental to 1,2,3, and 4.

Grants are not normally allowed for:

1   An additional facility (only for the adaptation of an existing fireplace).
2   Portable gas, electric or oil fires (only for installing gas or electric points).
3   Luxurious or expensive fittings.
4   The provision of additional fuel storage space.

It should be noted that the grant is allowed only for the expense incurred and that the claimant cannot include his own time and labour if he carried out the work himself. Also, any work qualifying for a grant under this Act will automatically be omitted from claims made under other Acts, such as improvement grants, etc.

Finally, if the claim is for removable appliances, and is made by the occupier rather than owner, only one half of the grant will be paid to start with; the other half will be payable after two years only if the appliances have not been removed from the dwelling.

Appendix II
Statutory and advisory bodies: useful addresses

Name	Address	Notes
British Flue and Chimney Manufacturers' Association	Unit 3 Phoenix House Phoenix Way Heston Middlesex TW5 9ND	Advisory pamphlet.
British Gas Corporation	59 Bryanston Street London W1 and 326 High Holborn London WC1V 7PT (12 regional offices)	Advice on the domestic use of gas, gas-fired heating, specialist contractors and safety. Free leaflets.
British Standards Institution (BSI)	2 Park Street London W1 (12 regional offices)	Advice and publications concerning the use of British Standards.
Building Centre	26 Store Street London WC1E 7BT (also regional offices)	Permanent exhibition, advisory service and information on building materials, products and services available. All major trades and suppliers are represented and can advise on local sources. SFAS's 'Living Fire Centre' is here as their central office and will advise on solid fuel use and appliances.
Chartered Institution of Building Services (CIBS) (formerly: Institution of Heating and Ventilating Engineers)	49 Cadogan Square London SW1 (11 regional branches)	Advice and publications on heating, ventilating and other building services.
Civic Trust	17 Carlton House Terrace London SW1Y 5AW	Advice and awards on design. Administer grant schemes for work in areas which are not outstanding conservation areas.
Council for the Protection of Rural England	4 Hobart Place London SW1	Advice on rural buildings.

Name	Address	Notes
Department of the Environment (DOE)	25 Savile Row London W1X 2BT	Responsible for listing and approval for alterations or demolition of buildings of special architectural or historic interest. Concerned with prevention of environmental pollution with special responsibility for clean air.
Federation of Master Builders	33 John Street London WC1N 2BB	Reputable medium to small builders are members; lists available.
Georgian Group	2 Chester Street London SW1X 7BB (similar Society in Scotland)	Advice on Georgian buildings.
Guild of Master Craftsmen Ltd	170 High Street Lewes East Sussex	Useful register of specialist contractors and craftsmen. Guide book of specialists in repair, restoration, renovation and conservation.
Heating and Ventilating Contractors Association (HVCA)	ESCA House 34 Palace Court Bayswater London W2 4JG	Advice on design and installation of central heating on their Home Heating Enquiry line (01 229 5543). List of members.
Historic Buildings Bureau	38 Ebury Street London SW1	Help in finding purchasers for historic buildings threatened with demolition.
Historic Houses Association	64 St James's Street London SW1A 1NT	Association of owners of historic houses.
Institution of Structural Engineers	11 Upper Belgrave Street London SW1	Advice on how to obtain structural engineering services in a particular area for a specific type of requirement.
National Fireplace Council Manufacturers' Association (formerly National Fireplace Manufacturers' Association and the Fireplace Tile Council)	P O Box 35 Stoke on Trent ST4 7NU	Information on products (trade).
National Home Improvement Council	26 Store Street London WC1E 7BT	Advice on home improvement, how to get professional services. Directory of reliable specialists.
National House Building Council	58 Portland Place London W1N 4BU	Advice and guidance on house building.
National Monuments Record	Fortress House 23 Savile Row London W1X 2HE (similar archives in Scotland and Wales)	Have photographic and drawn records of historic buildings. Index of records in private possession. Enquiry and advisory service available to the public.
National Society for Clean Air	136 North Street Brighton East Sussex BN1 1RG	Voluntary organization concerned with campaigning for clean air.

Name	Address	Notes
Royal Commission on Historical Monuments	23 Savile Row London W1X 2HE (similar bodies in Scotland and Wales)	Responsible for a county-by-county inventory survey of historical monuments.
Royal Institute of British Architects (RIBA)	66 Portland Place London W1N 4AD	Advice on how to obtain architectural services in a particular area for specific types of work. Free explanatory leaflet.
Scottish Tile, Fireplace and Domestic Heating Association	22 Hanover Street Edinburgh	Trade information.
Society for the Protection of Ancient Buildings (SPAB)	37 Spital Square London E1 6DY	Technical advice on repairs and alterations to historic buildings. Technical pamphlets.
The Solid Fuel Advisory Service (SFAS)	Coal House Lyon Road Harrow-on-the-Hill Middlesex HA1 2EX (London region) Head office: Hobart House Grosvenor Place London SW1X 7AE (8 regional offices, further local offices)	Useful advice, publications and site visits by experienced inspectors for general guidance concerning solid fuel use and appliances. See also the *Building Centre* for their 'Living Fire Centre'.
Solid Smokeless Fuel Federation	Devonshire House Church Street Sutton-in-Ashfield Nottinghamshire	Advice and information on the use and development of solid smokeless fuel.
Vernacular Architecture Group	Chy An Whyloryon Wigmore Leominster Herefordshire HR6 9UD	Advice on architectural matters concerning small houses and cottages.
Victorian Society	1 Priory Gardens London W4	Advice on Victorian buildings.
Wood burning Association of Retailers and Manufacturers (WARM)	P O Box 35 Stoke-on-Trent	Trade advice on the use of wood as fuel and on wood burning appliances

Appendix III
Product information sheets

The products listed in this section have been selected by the author from a wide range of similar ones available on the market. Many of the manufacturers named provide other product types, as well as those noted.

Further information on alternative manufacturers, retailers and products can be obtained from the Building Centre, the National Fireplace Council and the SFAS offices (see Appendix II for addresses).

1 Open fires

Name	Address	Notes
Baxi Burnall	Baxi Heating Brownedge Road Preston, Lancs PR5 6SN Tel: (0772) 36201	Suppliers of open-fire grates burning solid fuel with optional underfloor draught, back boilers and accessories (fire guards, overnight burning plates, canopies etc). Also supply an electric 'Baxi Fan' for solid floors.
Jetmaster Fires Limited	Winnall Manor Road Winnall Winchester, Hampshire SO23 8LT Tel: (0962) 51641	Multifuel open fires providing radiation and convection heat, can have a controlled burning facility for overnight burning.
Ouzledale Foundry Co Limited	P O Box 4 Long Ing Barnoldswick Colne, Lancs Tel: (0282) 813235	Manufacturers of open fire appliances, ('the Firemaster' range), grates and accessories.

2 Room heaters and cookers

Name	Address	Notes
Glynwed Appliances Limited	AGA Rayburn Division Ketley Telford, Shropshire TF1 3B2	Room heaters burning house coal smokelessly. Multi-fuel cookers which can also heat the domestic water.

Name	Address	Notes
Trianco Redfyre Limited	Stewart House Brookway Kingston Road Leatherhead, Surrey KT22 7LY Tel: (0372) 376453	Room heaters providing controlled heating where there is no space for a free-standing boiler. The Trianco Tallboy has been designed for buildings which do not have an existing chimney.
T I Parkray Limited	Park Foundry Belper, Derby DE5 1WE	Solid fuel room heaters which can also provide the hot water and run up to 10 radiators.

3 Wood-burning stoves

Name	Address	Notes
Hunter & Son (Mells) Limited	Frome, Somerset Tel: (0373) 812545	Established manufacturers of wood-burning stoves.
Jetmaster Fires Limited	Winnall Manor Road Winnall Winchester, Hampshire SO23 8LJ Tel: (0962) 51641	Suppliers of multifuel open fire/room heaters, of a double skin construction for a two way heating system: radiation and convention. Free trial facility.
The Stove Shop	Camden Lock Chalk Farm Road London NW1 Tel: (01) 969 9531	Antique continental stoves and restoration service.

4 Gas fires

NB Gas fires are not suitable for DIY and must be fitted by an authorized contractor within the provisions of the Gas Act 1972.

Name	Address	Notes
Kohlangaz Fire Co Limited	Kohlangaz House Kellaw Road Yarm Road Industrial Estate Darlington DL1 4YA Tel: (0325) 55438	Suppliers of coal/log effect gas fires, mostly recommended for appearance rather than heating efficiency.
Real Flame Log Fires	80 New King's Road Fulham London SW6 Tel: (01) 731 2704	Standard coal/log effect fires, also custom built. Installation service locally.

5 Materials

Name	Address	Notes
The Bulmer Brick and Tile Co Limited	Brickfields Bulmer (nr. Sudbury) Suffolk Tel: (0787) 29232	Manufacturers of special bricks for historic restoration, especially Tudor buildings.

Name	Address	Notes
Hewitt & Son (Fenton) Limited	Victoria Road Fenton Stoke-on-Trent, Staffs ST4 2HR Tel: (0782) 47151	Fireclay products (firebricks, fire tiles etc).
Kerner Greenwood & Co	Anne's House St Anne's Street King's Lynn, Norfolk PE30 1LU Tel: (0553) 2293/2371	'Feusol fire cement' suitable for setting fire bricks as it is resistant to heat.

6   Components (chimney terminals)

Name	Address	Notes
Red Bank Manufacturing Co Limited	Measham Burton-on-Trent, Staffs DE12 7EL Tel: (0530) 70333	Manufacturers of components for new fireplaces: Chimney pots, flue lining, fire backs, throat units, etc.
Aerocowl Marketing Limited	23 Station Street Belfast BT3 9DA Tel: (0232) 57481	Manufacture a chimney cowl which counteracts down-draught and ensures an equal pressure in the flue.
Strax Distribution Ltd	41b Brecknock Road London N7 0BT Tel: (01) 485 7056	Suppliers of electric chimney extractor fans, normally installed to cure smoking problems when alterations are impractical. *NB* have no standby in the case of power cuts.

7   Components (maintenance/improvements)

Name	Address	Notes
Marshall & Parsons Limited	1111 London Road Leigh on Sea, Essex SS9 3JL Tel: (0702) 710404	Suppliers of Draughtmaster, a one-way air inlet grille useful in situations when air starvation is causing a smoking fire.
Hydrachem Limited	Daux Road Billingshurst, West Sussex RH14 9UN Tel: (040 381) 4332	Main product: Flue Free – a powder designed to combat the formation of tar and creosote deposits, when sprinkled over a low burning fire. It does not eliminate the need for sweeping but it ensures a more efficient clean. Other products: Glass or fireplace cleaners (for removing smoke stains) Stove polish Stove paint (for use in high temperature and corrosive conditions).

8 Flue liners

Name	Address	Notes
True Flue Division Marley Buildings Limited	Shurdington Nr Cheltenham Gloucester GL51 5UE Tel: (0242) 862551	Chimney accessories and Class I liners. Typex – gas flues made of hollow precast concrete blocks. True flue – twin wall system.
Park Sectional Insulating Co Limited	244 Romford Road Forest Gate London E7 9HZ Tel: (01) 534 7695	Parkabest Universal prefabricated insulated chimney sections consisting of a stainless steel lining, moulded mineral fibre insulation and galvanized steel outer casing. Parkaflue – ceramic lining.
Stranks-Monodraught Flues Limited	Unit 1 Binders Yard Cryers Hill High Wycombe, Bucks Tel: (0494) 713413	Balanced flue chimney system supplied as a set of precast blocks.
Red Bank Manufacturing Co Limited	Atherstone Road Measham Burton-on-Trent, DE12 7EL Tel: (0530) 70333	Comprehensive range of clay flue linings, of circular or square section to BS 1181 in red terracotta buff fireclays in glazed or ceramic glazed.

9 Accessories

Name	Address	Notes
J.D. Beardmore & Co Limited	Field End Road Ruislip, Middlesex HA4 OQG Tel: (01) 864 6811	Brass and cast-iron reproduction accessories. Firebacks are manufactured using a selection of antique casting patterns ranging from Tudor to 18th century.
Kingsworthy Foundry	Kingsworthy Winchester, Hampshire Tel: (0962) 883776	Reproduction Georgian grates finished in old pewter among others.
Samuel Heath	Cobden Works Leopold Street Birmingham B12 OUJ Tel: (021) 772 2303	Reproduction firescreens, fire tools fenders, coal buckets etc.

10 Period fireplaces/Antiques

Name	Address	Notes
Crowthers of Syon Lodge	Busch Corner London Road Isleworth, Middlesex Tel: (01) 560 7978 also at 6 Old Bond Street London W1 Tel: (01) 493 8688	Specialists in architectural antiques with a tradition in original chimney-pieces. Complete interiors, such as entire panelled rooms are acquired and adapted if necessary, to suit a new location. Installation service available.

Name	Address	Notes
The London Architectural Salvage and Supply Company Limited	Mark Street (off Paul Street) London EC2 Tel: (01) 739 0448/9	Housed in a restored church saved from demolition, the company supplies a variety of original architectural fixtures and fittings and has a stock of original fire surrounds of marble, timber or cast iron, dating from C17, C18 and C19. Elizabethan and rare C18 examples stocked at an associate company in Hampstead: (01) 435 0052.
Architectural Heritage	Boddington Manor Boddington nr Cheltenham, Glos Tel: Cheltenham 68741	Architectural salvage in stock sometimes includes fire surrounds etc.

11 Period fireplaces/Reproduction surrounds

Name	Address	Notes
G. Jackson & Sons Limited	Rathbone Works Rainville Road Hammersmith London W6 9HD Tel: (01) 385 6616	Founded in 1780 (John and Robert Adam were among the main customers), the company specializes in fibrous plaster and woodwork interior decorations, among which a range of 24 Georgian design chimney pieces is available.
Acquisitions (Fireplaces) Limited	269 Camden High Street London NW1 7BX Tel: (01) 485 4955	Specialists in original and reproduction Victorian/Edwardian cast-iron and pine fireplace surrounds some with hand decorated tile inserts. Also available are fireside accessories and a supply/installation service for Kohlangaz coal/log effect gas fires.

Bibliography

The bibliography is divided into two parts covering historical and technical works respectively.

Part 1 Historical references

Addy, S.O., *The Evolution of the English House*, Swan Sonnenschein & Co., Ltd, 1905

Barley, M.W., *The English Farm House and Cottage*, Routledge & Kegan Paul, 1961

Bernan, W., *Warming and Ventilating*, Bell, 1884

Clavering, Robert, *Essay on Chimney Construction*, 1779

Cunnington, Pamela, *How Old is Your House?*, Alpha Books, 1980

Eckstein, G.F., *Eckstein on Chimneys*, John Weale, 1852

Edwards, Frederick, *Our Domestic Fireplaces*, Robert Hardwicke, 1865

Evelyn, John, *Fumifugium*, 1661, published in facsimile by National Smoke Abatement Society, 1933

Fletcher, Valentine, *Chimney Pots and Stacks*, Centaur Press, 1968

Harris, Eileen (Victoria and Albert Museum) *Keeping Warm*, HMSO, 1982

Harrison, Rev. William, *Elizabethan England*, Withington L.Ed, Scott-London, 1899

Knowles, C.C. and P.H. Pitt, *The History of the Building Regulations in London 1189–1972*. The Architectural Press, 1972

Lander, Hugh, *House and Cottage Interiors*, Acanthus Books, 1982

Lloyd, Nathaniel, *History of the English House*, The Architectural Press, 1931, reprinted 1975, 1979

Maccy, F.W., *Specification*, 1899

Neve, Richard, *The City and Country Purcherser*, 1703, reprinted by David and Charles, 1969

Nicholson, Peter, *Dictionary of the Science and Practice of Architecture, Building, Etc*, 1797

Putnam, J. Pickering, *The Open Fireplace in all Ages*. James R. Osgood & Co.(Boston), 1882

Count Rumford, Essay X, Part 1, T. Cadell, J.R. & W. Davies, 1799

Salzman, L.F., *Building in England Down to 1540*, Oxford University Press, 1952

Shuffrey, L.A. *The English Fireplace*, B.T. Batsford, 1912

Sotheby's Great Stove Event Auction Catalogue, Sotheby's, 1979

Turner, T. Hudson, *Some Accounts of Domestic Architecture in England. From the Conquest to the End of the Thirteenth Century*, J.H. Parker (Oxford), 1851

Ware, Isaac, *A Complete Body of Architecture*, 1756

West, Trudy, *The Fireplace in the Home*, David and Charles (Canada), 1976

Wood, Margaret, *The English Mediaeval House*, Ferndale Editions, 1981

Woodforde, John, *The Diary of a Country Parson 1758–1781*, Oxford University Press, 1924

Wright, Lawrence, *Home Fires Building*, Routledge & Kegan Paul, 1964

Part 2   Technical

Bidwell, T.G., *The Conservation of Brick Buildings*, Brick Development Association, 1977

Bonell, D.G.R. and W.R. Pippard, National Building Studies Bulletin No 9, *Some Common Defects in Brickwork*, HMSO, 1950

British Flue and Chimney Manufacturers' Association, *A General Guide on Flues and Chimneys for Domestic Solid Fuel and Wood-burning Appliances*, 1982

Burberry, Peter and Arthur Aldersey-Williams, 'Domestic Heating', *Architects' Journal*, August–September, 1977

Curtis, Christopher and Donald Post, *Be Your Own Chimney Sweep*, Garden Way Publishing, 1979

Davey, A., Bob Heath, Desmond Hodges, Roy Milne, Mandy Palmer, *The Care and Conservation of Georgian Houses*, Edinburgh New Town Conservation Committee/The Architectural Press, 1978

DoE/PSA, Advisory Leaflet No 50, *Chimneys for Domestic Boilers*, HMSO, 1975

Eldridge, H.J./DoE/PSA, *Common Defects in Buildings*, HMSO

Garner, J.F. *Alteration or Conversion of Houses*, Oyez Practice Notes, Oyez Publishing, 1981

Lead Development Association, *Lead Sheet in Building*, 1978

Lloyd, Nathaniel, *Building Craftsmanship in Brick and Tile and in Stone Slates*, Cambridge University Press, 1929

McGuigan, Dermot, *Burning Wood*, Prism Press, 1979

Melville, Ian A. and Ian A. Gordon, *The Repair and Maintenance of Houses*, The Estates Gazette Ltd, 1973, 1979

Ministry of Public Building and Works, Advisory Leaflet No 58, *Inserting a Damp-proof Course*, HMSO, 1970

Mitchell's Building Construction/Jack Stroud Foster, *Structure and Fabric*, Part 1, B.T. Batsford, 1973

National Building Agency, *Brickwork, Domestic Fireplaces and Chimneys*, Brick Development Association, 1981

National Building Agency, *Easy Guide to Solid Fuel and Oil Heating in Housing*, Building Design, Nov, 1979

Porteous, Andrew, *Wood—the Alternative Fuel*, Hickory House Press, 1978

Ransom, W.H., *Building Failures*, E. & F.N. Spon, 1981

Roshfield Publications Ltd, *The Fireplace Book*, 1980

Solid Fuel Advisory Service, *The Architect's Compendium*, 'Solid Fuel Heating'

Solid Fuel Advisory Service, *Curing Chimney Troubles*

Solid Fuel Advisory Service, *Approved Domestic Solid Fuel*

Solid Fuel Advisory Service, *The Free Inset Installation*

Williams, G.B.A., *Chimneys in Old Buildings*, Technical Pamphlet 3, SPAB, 1976

Codes of Practice and British Standards

CP121 Brick and block masonry

CP131 Chimneys and flues for domestic appliances burning solid fuel

CP403 (1974) Installation of domestic heating and cooking appliances burning solid fuel

CP332 Town gas space heaters – domestic installation

BS

1251:1970 Specification for open fireplace components

1181 Flue linings and terminals – clay

567, 835 Asbestos cement flue pipes

715 Sheet metal lining for gas

5854 Flues and flue structures code

5440 Flues for gas appliances

3572 Chimney access fittings

3678 Chimney access hooks

4543 Factory made insulated chimneys (revised 1976)

4207 Monolithic chimney linings (revised 1982)

4076 Steel chimneys

3456 Electric appliances – safety

5864, 5986 Gas fired appliances

5990 Forced convection air heaters

1250 Town gas space heaters – domestic

5449 Heating domestic premises

2028, 1364 Precast concrete blocks

This information was correct at the time of going to press. Names, addresses and product specifications may since have changed.

Illustration Credits

Chapter 1

1.1 to 1.3b, *RMcD*
1.4 to 1.5c, *AMcD*
1.6, *NMR*
1.7, 1.8a, *RMcD*
1.8b, *NMR*
1.9, *RMcD*
1.9b, *NMR*
1.9c, *NMR*
1.10a to 1.11d, *RMcD*
1.12a, *NMR*
1.12b, *MRL*
1.13a, *RMcD*
1.13b, *MP*
1.13c, *SI*
1.13d, *SI*
1.14, *AMcD*
1.15, *NMR*
1.16a, 1.16b, *RMcD*
1.17, *MRL*
1.18, *MRL*
1.19 (2 of), *AMcD*
1.20a, 1.20b, *MRL*
1.20c, *RMcD*
1.21, *RIBA*
1.22, *NMR*
1.23, *RMcD*
1.24a, *C I + Soane*
1.24b, *C I*
1.24c, *AMcD*
1.25a, 1.25b, *A*
1.25c, *MRL*
1.26a, *RMcD*
1.26b, *RMcD*
1.27, *RIBA*
1.28, *MRL*
1.29, 1.30, *RIBA*
1.31, *AMcD*

Chapter 2

2.1, *MRL*
2.2, *NMR*
2.3, *NMR*
2.4a to 2.9, *RMcD*
2.10, *WG*
2.11, *AMcD*
2.12a to 2.15c, *RMcD*
2.16, *RIBA*
2.17, *RMcD*
2.18, *RMcD*

Chapter 3

3.1, *AMcD*
3.2, 3.3, 3.4, *RMcD*
3.5, *NMR*
3.6, 3.7a, 3.7b, 3.8, *RMcD*
3.9, *AMcD*
3.10, 3.11, *RMcD*
3.12a & 3.13b, *CT*
3.13, *MRL*
3.14 to 3.16d, *RMcD*

Chapter 4

4.1 to 4.5, *RMcD*
4.6, *AMcD*
4.7, *RMcD*
4.8, *AMcD*
4.9, *NS*
4.10a, b, c, *RMcD*
4.11 to 4.16, *RMcD*
4.17, *MRL*
4.18, 4.19, *RMcD*

Chapter 6

6.1 to 6.6f, *RMcD*
6.6g, 6.6h, *AMcD*
6.7, 6.8, 6.9, *RMcD*

Chapter 7

7.1, 7.3, 7.4, 7.5, *RMcD*
7.2, *MRL*

Appendix

1, *RMcD*

Key to Credits

RMcD, Roxana McDonald
AMcD, Alastair McDonald
NMR, National Monuments
    Record
MRL, Institute of Agricultural
    History and Museum of
    English Rural Life, University
    of Reading
MP, Michael Peach
SI, Syndication International Ltd
RIBA, British Architectural
    Library/RIBA
CI, Courtauld Institute of Art
Soane, Soane Museum
A, Aquisitions, 269 Camden
    High Street, London NW1
WG, Wolverhampton Art
    Gallery
CT, Civic Trust Library
NS, Nicholas Sargeant

Index

157